Shulamith Lala Ashenberg
Larry Harrison
Editors

International Aspects of Social Work Practice in the Addictions

International Aspects of Social Work Practice in the Addictions has been co-published simultaneously as *Journal of Social Work Practice in the Addictions,* Volume 2, Numbers 3/4 2002

Pre-publication
REVIEWS,
COMMENTARIES,
EVALUATIONS . . .

"**P**rovides detailed descriptions and analyses of a wide variety of approaches to helping people who experience drug and alcohol problems in the United States, Israel, Singapore, and a range of European countries. . . . Particularly useful for the reader who wishes to place their own interventions and agency policies into a much wider and broader context, which opens up possibilities of a whole range of approaches to the complexities that surround drug and alcohol problems."

Stewart Collins, MA
Senior Lecturer in Social Work
University of Wales

International Aspects
of Social Work Practice
in the Addictions

International Aspects of Social Work Practice in the Addictions has been co-published simultaneously as *Journal of Social Work Practice in the Addictions*, Volume 2, Numbers 3/4 2002.

learning network
west

The *Journal of Social Work Practice in the Addictions*[TM] Monographic "Separates"

Below is a list of "separates," which in serials librarianship means a special issue simultaneously published as a special journal issue or double-issue *and* as a "separate" hardbound monograph. (This is a format which we also call a "DocuSerial.")

"Separates" are published because specialized libraries or professionals may wish to purchase a specific thematic issue by itself in a format which can be separately cataloged and shelved, as opposed to purchasing the journal on an on-going basis. Faculty members may also more easily consider a "separate" for classroom adoption.

"Separates" are carefully classified separately with the major book jobbers so that the journal tie-in can be noted on new book order slips to avoid duplicate purchasing.

You may wish to visit Haworth's Website at . . .

http://www.HaworthPress.com

. . . to search our online catalog for complete tables of contents of these separates and related publications.

You may also call 1-800-HAWORTH (outside US/Canada: 607-722-5857), or Fax 1-800-895-0582 (outside US/Canada: 607-771-0012), or e-mail at:

getinfo@haworthpressinc.com

International Aspects of Social Work Practice in the Addictions, edited by Shulamith Lala Ashenberg Straussner, DSW, CAS, and Larry Harrison, MA CQSW (Vol. 2, No. 3/4, 2002). *"Provides valuable insight into one of the most significant changes in social life during the last fifty years and indicates some of the likely direction for changes in the first half of the twenty-first century." (Tony Clamp, DipCouns, DipSW, MA, Lecturer in Applied Social Studies, University of Durham, United Kingdom)*

Neurobiology of Addictions: Implications for Clinical Practice, edited by Richard T. Spence, PhD, MSSW, Diana M. DiNitto, PhD and Shulamith Lala Ashenberg Straussner, DSW, CAS (Vol. 1, No. 3, 2001). *Presents the neurobiological theories of addiction in a psychosocial context and connects the theoretical information with practical applications.*

International Aspects of Social Work Practice in the Addictions

Shulamith Lala Ashenberg Straussner
Larry Harrison
Editors

International Aspects of Social Work Practice in the Addictions has been co-published simultaneously as *Journal of Social Work Practice in the Addictions*, Volume 2, Numbers 3/4 2002.

THSWPP

The Haworth Social Work Practice Press
An Imprint of
The Haworth Press, Inc.
New York • London • Oxford

Published by

The Haworth Social Work Practice Press, 10 Alice Street, Binghamton, NY 13904-1580 USA

The Haworth Social Work Practice Press is an imprint of The Haworth Press, Inc., 10 Alice Street, Binghamton, NY 13904-1580 USA.

International Aspects of Social Work Practice in the Addictions has been co-published simultaneously as *Journal of Social Work Practice in the Addictions*, Volume 2, Numbers 3/4 2002.

The development, preparation, and publication of this work has been undertaken with great care. However, the publisher, employees, editors, and agents of The Haworth Press and all imprints of The Haworth Press, Inc., including The Haworth Medical Press® and The Pharmaceutical Products Press®, are not responsible for any errors contained herein or for consequences that may ensue from use of materials or information contained in this work. Opinions expressed by the author(s) are not necessarily those of The Haworth Press, Inc.

Cover design by Jennifer M. Gaska.

Library of Congress Cataloging-in-Publication Data

International aspects of social work practice in the addictions/ editors, Shulamith Lala Ashenberg Straussner Larry Harrison, editors.
     p. cm.
    "Co-published simultaneously as Journal of Social Work Practice in the Addictions, volume 2, numbers 3/4, 2002."
    Includes bibliographical references and index.
    ISBN 0-7890-1996-5 (case. : alk. paper) – ISBN 0-7890-1997-3 (soft: alk. paper)
    1. Social work with narcotic addicts–Cross-cultural studies. 2. Substance abuse–Treatment–Cross–cultural studies. I. Straussner, Shulamith Lala Ashenberg. II. Harrison, Larry, 1946-. III. Journal of social work practice in the addictions.
HV5801.I558 2003
362.29′186–dc21
                                                  2003002284

Indexing, Abstracting & Website/Internet Coverage

This section provides you with a list of major indexing & abstracting services. That is to say, each service began covering this periodical during the year noted in the right column. Most Websites which are listed below have indicated that they will either post, disseminate, compile, archive, cite or alert their own Website users with research-based content from this work. (This list is as current as the copyright date of this publication.)

(continued)

Special Bibliographic Notes related to special journal issues (separates) and indexing/abstracting:

- indexing/abstracting services in this list will also cover material in any "separate" that is co-published simultaneously with Haworth's special thematic journal issue or DocuSerial. Indexing/abstracting usually covers material at the article/chapter level.
- monographic co-editions are intended for either non-subscribers or libraries which intend to purchase a second copy for their circulating collections.
- monographic co-editions are reported to all jobbers/wholesalers/approval plans. The source journal is listed as the "series" to assist the prevention of duplicate purchasing in the same manner utilized for books-in-series.
- to facilitate user/access services all indexing/abstracting services are encouraged to utilize the co-indexing entry note indicated at the bottom of the first page of each article/chapter/contribution.
- this is intended to assist a library user of any reference tool (whether print, electronic, online, or CD-ROM) to locate the monographic version if the library has purchased this version but not a subscription to the source journal.

International Aspects of Social Work Practice in the Addictions

CONTENTS

ABOUT THE EDITORS

Shulamith Lala Ashenberg Straussner, DSW, CSW, CEAP, BCD, CAS, is Professor at New York University Shirley M. Ehrenkranz School of Social Work and Coordinator of their Post-Master's Program in the Treatment of Alcohol and Drug Abusing Clients (TADAC). She has been involved in the field of addictions for over 25 years as a clinician, supervisor, researcher, policy analyst, and educator, and has made hundreds of presentations in the U.S. and abroad. Dr. Straussner is past Chair of the Alcohol, Tobacco, and Other Drugs Section of the National Association of Social Workers and a board member of New York State Institute for Professional Development in the Addictions.

Dr. Straussner has written numerous publications dealing with substance abuse and with occupational social work and EAPs. Among her ten books are *Occupational Social Work* (Haworth); *Clinical Work With Substance Abusing Clients*; *Gender and Addictions: Men and Women in Treatment*; *Ethnocultural Factors in Substance Abuse Treatment*; and the *Handbook on Addiction Treatment for Women* (with Stephanie Brown). She is also the founding editor of the *Journal of Social Work Practice in the Addictions*.

Dr. Straussner has been Visiting Professor at several universities in Israel and in Siberia, Russia, and has served as a consultant to public and private agencies and organizations in the U.S. and abroad. She has a private clinical and supervisory practice in New York City.

Larry Harrison, MA, CQSW, is former Co-Director of the World Health Organization's U.K. Collaborating Centre on Substance Problems, based at the Universities of York and Hull in England. He was the University of Hull's Reader in Addiction Studies and Head of the School of Community and Health Studies in the Faculty of Health. Mr. Harrison is currently an Honorary Research Fellow at the University of Kent in Canterbury, England, where he conducts research into the epidemiology of alcohol and drug dependence.

Mr. Harrison has published extensively on issues of prevention and policy in relation to substance misuse. His books include *Alcohol Policies: Responsibilities and Relationships in British Government*; *Alcohol and Disadvantage Amongst the Irish in England*; *Substance Misuse: Designing Social Work Training*; and *Alcohol Problems in the Community*. He has been Visiting Professor at the University of Northern Iowa and an advisor to the World Health Organization, to a cabinet office committee of the British government, and to the U.K. Central Council for Education and Training in Social Work.

International Aspects
of Social Work Practice
in the Addictions

International Aspects of Social Work Practice in the Addictions has been co-published simultaneously as *Journal of Social Work Practice in the Addictions*, Volume 2, Numbers 3/4 2002.

Introduction

The abuse of and addiction to alcohol and other drugs, and the resulting negative impact on individuals, families, communities and society as a whole, are a world-wide phenomena. Nonetheless, the substances that are abused, the scope of the problems, the social reactions, and the role of professionals in addressing these issues are unique to each country. The way in which particular therapies gain prestige and come to be seen as effective solutions to problems is not simply dependent on scientific evidence, but on political, organisational, economic and cultural factors. An intervention that is demonstrably cost effective can be rejected because it is ideologically unacceptable, or because allocating additional resources to a stigmatised group is unpopular. On the other hand, a treatment that has no apparent scientific validity, like the practice of conducting detoxification with the aid of a herbal emetic in rural Thailand, may be extremely effective if it fits with local people's expectations and beliefs about the nature of the problem.

We gain a more critical understanding of the socioeconomic and cultural influences on treatment systems by studying social work practices in other countries. A comparative international perspective helps us to reflect on which aspects of our response may be successful; which may be less important than we imagine; and which taken-for-granted elements seem distinctly odd from the perspective of another culture. This special volume is dedicated, therefore, to examining current social work practice in the addictions in a number of different countries. There are articles from contributors in Germany, Ireland, Israel, Singapore, the Nether-

[Haworth co-indexing entry note]: "Introduction." Harrison, Larry, and Shulamith Lala Ashenberg Straussner. Co-published simultaneously in *Journal of Social Work Practice in the Addictions* (The Haworth Social Work Practice Press, an imprint of The Haworth Press, Inc.) Vol. 2, No. 3/4, 2002, pp. 1-5; and: *International Aspects of Social Work Practice in the Addictions* (ed: Shulamith Lala Ashenberg Straussner, and Larry Harrison) The Haworth Social Work Practice Press, an imprint of The Haworth Press, Inc., 2002, pp. 1-5. Single or multiple copies of this article are available for a fee from The Haworth Document Delivery Service [1-800-HAWORTH, 9:00 a.m. - 5:00 p.m. (EST). E-mail address: getinfo@haworthpressinc.com].

1

lands and the United States, while the dialogue on the question of legalizing illicit drugs, features discussants from Australia, the United Kingdom (UK) and the United States (US). The exploration of substance abuse among immigrants from the Former Soviet Union by three social workers, Isralowitz, Straussner, and Vogt and a psychiatrist, Chtenguelov, from four different countries points out not only the growing role of social workers as researchers and the need for interdisciplinary collaboration in this field, but also the need for increasing our understanding regarding the abuse of substances from a cross-cultural and social perspective.

It is clear from the contributions to this special volume that there are large areas of consensus alongside areas of disagreement. There is a fair measure of agreement, for example, that addiction problems are a complex biopsychosocial phenomenon, and that they do respond to intervention. All of the nations represented in the articles and discussion in this collection share the experience of rapid social change accompanied by rising rates of psychoactive substance problems over the last half a century.

Alcohol consumption has risen by about 60% world-wide since the end of World War II (Raistrick, Hodgson, & Ritson, 1999), and illicit drug consumption and related problems have grown exponentially. In the UK, for example, the number seeking help for opiate and/or cocaine dependence increased by a factor of 122 over a forty year period: from under 350 in 1958 to over 43,000 in the year 1996 (Corkery, 1997). In 1958, the use of illicit drugs such as cannabis was relatively rare in England, even in major ports like London or Liverpool. By 1997, surveys indicated that *one in three* UK adults of working age had used an illicit drug at some time in their lives, and about 15 percent of those aged 16 to 29 had used an illicit drug in the previous month (Ramsay & Spiller, 1997). A change in social habits on this scale is a cultural shift of seismic proportions, and the same story can be repeated in many other countries around the world.

As Elizabeth Zelvin notes in her introduction to the panel discussion, different countries have responded to this phenomenal growth in problematic substance use in different ways. Historically, there were major differences in alcohol policies, from Prohibition in the US, and the use of rigorous supply side controls in the UK, to the more *laissez faire* policies that existed in Germany, France and Southern Europe. These differences have attenuated in recent years, as market-oriented alcohol policies, characterised by a light regulatory touch, have gained ground everywhere, and controls on the price, availability and promotion of alcoholic beverages have been liberalised.

Where cocaine, opiates, cannabis and other psychoactive substances are concerned, there has been rather more unanimity, fostered by a series of international treaties and negotiations over drug controls. The trend in Australian policy, which James Barber identifies in his contribution to the panel discussion, is shared by many other nations: More substances are subjected to prohibitions and controls; the scope and number of offences are increased and made easier to prove in court; the severity of statutory penalties has increased; and the enforcement and investigative powers of the police are being extended.

As the twenty first century dawns, however, there is a growing lack of support for this emphasis on supply side policies. In Australia and the UK, critics point to the lack of success achieved by law enforcement, and look towards countries like the Netherlands, Switzerland, and parts of Germany for examples of radical policy alternatives. Even in the US, the country most committed to suppressing the international trade in illicit drugs, there is some disquiet. As Diana DiNitto notes in her review of addiction social work in the US, there is concern over the barriers to treatment access that have arisen as a result of the War on Drugs.

Given the complexity of these issues, social workers in all countries will identify with Bill Coleman's *cri-de-cour* that as someone who has seen both sides of the fence, as a former U.S. Federal Special Agent and as a social worker currently treating people with substance problems, he has "come full circle several times about what is needed." There are no simple solutions. The countries represented here differ substantially over how much emphasis is placed on supply side as opposed to demand side measures, with Singapore, as indicated by Mohd Maliki Osman using the death penalty for convicted drug smugglers, while the Netherlands tolerates the sale of narcotics in an old age home. Nations also differ in the priority given to harm minimisation. Germany and the Netherlands have pioneered the use of injection rooms, as seen in the photograph on the end page. Here street users can inject drugs in sterile conditions, with first aid available should they overdose and, in some settings, with social workers and social work students on-site should any addict wish to talk or need help with concrete services. At the other extreme, in the US–the country that arguably adopted harm minimisation first, following Dole and Nyswander's experiments on the 'blockading' effect of methadone in the early 1960s–DiNitto reminds us that syringe exchange schemes remain illegal in most jurisdictions.

It is clear, however, that national responses cannot simply be categorised as tough or soft on drugs, based on the prominence given to their criminal justice system: instead, they vary along a series of dimensions. There is, for example, considerable variation in the centrality of social work intervention to the national response. Peleg-Oren, Rahav and Teichman show that where social workers have had the study of substance problems integrated into their professional qualifying training, as in Israel, they are more likely to see intervention in substance problems as part of their role. In Israel, the US and Germany, many social workers are in the forefront of attempts to help people with substance problems, including involvement at the national policy level. While in Ireland, the Netherlands and Singapore the role of social workers are more marginal and it is harder to bring the subject into the mainstream of social work education and training.

There are also marked cross-national differences in the form in which social work intervention takes. In the Netherlands and Germany, there has been more of an emphasis on urban regeneration, on anti-poverty programs, and on community work, rather than on clinical social work. Ireland is in transition, Shane Butler argues, from an earlier US based model, which stressed individual counselling, towards a European approach that embraces more of an environmental focus.

However, as James Barber points out, policies can be adopted in inconsistent and even contradictory ways. In 1998 the Prime Minister of Australia publicly endorsed a *zero tolerance* approach to illicit drug use, Barber notes, although this was in direct opposition to Australia's policy of harm minimisation. Similarly, it should not be assumed that a heightened awareness among policy makers of the way in which poverty and environmental disadvantage raise the risk of substance problems among vulnerable groups will automatically lead to an increased role for social workers. While in Israel a growing awareness of the social dimensions of problematic substance use seems to have been accompanied by social work becoming the "pivotal profession in the field," in the Netherlands the policies on harm minimisation and on normalisation, described by de Koning and de Kwant, have given less of a role to the social work profession than might be expected. If, for historical reasons, the status of the social work profession is insecure, it seems that the adoption of broadly based prevention and harm reduction programmes simply reinforce the marginal position of the profession.

Whatever the differences in the perspectives on the nature of the problem, and in social policies, institutional practices, sources of funding and social work methods that are evident in the contributions to this special volume, there is an encouraging measure of agreement. Social workers in all countries seem to share an underlying sense of the tragedy that addiction can so often mean to people, and to be united in their conviction that social work intervention can make a difference.

Larry Harrison
Kirkburn, England

Shulamith Lala Ashenberg Straussner
New York, NY, USA

May 20, 2002

REFERENCES

Corkery, J. M. (1997). *Statistics of Drug Addicts Notified to the Home Office, United Kingdom, 1996*. Issue 22/97. London: Home Office.

Raistrick, D., Hodgson, R., & Ritson, B. (Eds.). (1999). *Tackling Alcohol Together*. London: Free Association Books.

Ramsay, M. and Spiller, J. (1997). *Drug Misuse Declared in 1996: Latest Results from the British Crime Survey*. London: HMSO.

War and Peace:
Social Work and the State
of Chemical Dependency Treatment
in the United States

Diana M. DiNitto

SUMMARY. In recent decades, treatment for alcohol and drug problems in the United States has been influenced by a number of factors. This article discusses several of these factors, including the "War on Drugs," with its emphasis on law enforcement and interdiction, and managed health care, which has compromised access to treatment. In spite of these factors, the U.S. invests a goodly amount in alcohol and drug prevention and treatment services and research. Efforts are being made to ensure that research findings are being translated into improved clinical practice. Among the controversial issues in the treatment arena are recent efforts by the Bush administration to promote public funding of faith- or religious-based groups in delivering chemical dependency services. Social workers commonly see people with alcohol and drug

Diana M. DiNitto, PhD, is Cullen Trust Centennial Professor in Alcohol Studies and Education, The University of Texas at Austin School of Social Work, Austin, Texas (E-mail: ddinitto@mail.utexas.edu).

[Haworth co-indexing entry note]: "War and Peace: Social Work and the State of Chemical Dependency Treatment in the United States." DiNitto, Diana M. Co-published simultaneously in *Journal of Social Work Practice in the Addictions* (The Haworth Social Work Practice Press, an imprint of The Haworth Press, Inc.) Vol. 2, No. 3/4, 2002, pp. 7-29; and: *International Aspects of Social Work Practice in the Addictions* (ed: Shulamith Lala Ashenberg Straussner, and Larry Harrison) The Haworth Social Work Practice Press, an imprint of The Haworth Press, Inc., 2002, pp. 7-29. Single or multiple copies of this article are available for a fee from The Haworth Document Delivery Service [1-800-HAWORTH, 9:00 a.m. - 5:00 p.m. (EST). E-mail address: getinfo@haworthpressinc.com].

problems in their practices, but only a small number of social workers are well prepared to treat this group of clients. *[Article copies available for a fee from The Haworth Document Delivery Service: 1-800-HAWORTH. E-mail address: <getinfo@haworthpressinc.com> Website: <http://www.HaworthPress.com> © 2002 by The Haworth Press, Inc. All rights reserved.]*

KEYWORDS. Addiction treatment in U.S., chemical or substance dependency, substance abuse, social work, policy, war on drugs

INTRODUCTION

This article considers the state of substance abuse treatment and related issues in the United States (U.S.) and their relevance to social work practice. The material is grouped under five headings: (1) the "war on drugs," (2) access to chemical dependency treatment, (3) transferring advancements in research and treatment technology, (4) keeping the faith, and (5) social work credentialing and chemical dependency treatment.

THE WAR ON DRUGS

The "war on drugs" is the most recognized description of the U.S. approach to drug problems. The U.S. has waged this war since it began fashioning the Harrison Narcotics Act of 1914. The current war effort began during the Nixon administration (see Gray, 1998). During the 1980s, President Ronald Reagan escalated this effort, culminating in the establishment of the Office of National Drug Control Policy (ONDCP). ONDCP's director, dubbed the "drug czar," became a Cabinet level official (top presidential adviser). For recent U.S. presidents, alcohol and drugs became personal as well as public policy issues. The Betty Ford Center, probably the most highly visible addiction treatment center in the world, is named for the wife of a former president who has dealt with her own addiction. Former President Bill Clinton admitted trying marijuana, and members of his own family have had alcohol and cocaine problems. Current President George W. Bush has a conviction for driving under the influence of alcohol and has chosen to abstain completely from drinking alcohol. He has declined to discuss other drug use, although both his daughter and his niece have had legal problems due to the use of alcohol or drugs.

Crime and Punishment

The nation's current $20 billion federal drug control budget (ONDCP, 2001) may seem astonishing to those in other countries. During the administrations of former Presidents Bush and Clinton, about two-thirds of the national drug control budget went to law enforcement and interdiction, and one-third to prevention, treatment, education, and research (ONDCP, 1999). This allocation contradicts what we know about the success of "supply" versus "demand" side strategies. There is a savings of about $12 in criminal justice, health care, and related costs for every $1 spent on treatment (National Institute on Drug Abuse [NIDA], 1999). Nevertheless, a 2001 national opinion poll conducted found that while 74% of Americans feel that the U.S. is losing the drug war, 52% said that the government should emphasize "stopping drug importation" (Pew Research Center, 2001). Only 36% thought that drug treatment should be emphasized.

Drug crimes are the single greatest contributor to the phenomenal increase in incarceration in the U.S. According to the ONDCP (1998), between 1985 and 1995, almost three-quarters of the increase in the federal prison population was due to drug offenses, and the state prison population incarcerated for drug-law violations increased by 478%. In 1999 alone, there were more than 1.5 million arrests for drug violations (ONDCP, 2001). Of all drug law violations, 80% were for possession of illegal drugs, and drug and alcohol offenses accounted for nearly one-third of the nation's arrests. Meanwhile, conservative estimates are that about 13 to 16 million Americans need substance abuse treatment, but that only about 3 million receive it, resulting in a large "treatment gap" (Center for Substance Abuse Treatment [CSAT], 2000).

In an effort to blend criminal justice and treatment approaches, more substance or chemical dependency treatment is being conducted in jails and prisons and through criminal justice diversion programs (see Coffey, Mark, King, Harwood, McKusick, Genuardi et al., 2001; McNeece & DiNitto, 1998). A substantial number of probationers and parolees also participate in some type of chemical dependency treatment. An example of in-prison treatment is the 520-bed New Vision modified therapeutic community for male inmates located in Kyle, Texas. The facility is also notable because it is operated by a private, for-profit company, the Wackenhut Corrections Corporation. Privatization of public services has become common (see DiNitto, 2000), and chemical dependency treatment professionals find themselves working in a variety of venues.

Reforming Welfare and Education

Many policies in addition to incarceration constitute the drug war (see DiNitto, 2000). The Americans with Disabilities Act of 1990 provides employment protections to those with past alcohol and other drug problems. However, it does not provide those who currently use illegal drugs or whose job performance is impaired by alcohol with the same level of employment protections as offered to individuals with other disabilities (see de Miranda, 1990; Program on Employment and Disability, 2001). Though many alcoholics and addicts have paid into the Social Security Disability Insurance (SSDI) program while employed, alcohol and drug addiction do not qualify as disabilities in this program. Alcohol and drug addiction are also not qualifying conditions for the nation's public assistance program for poor people with disabilities called Supplemental Security Income (SSI) (see Coffey et al., 2001; Committee on Ways and Means, 1998, pp. 302-304; Conklin, 1997; DiNitto, 2000; McNeece & DiNitto, 1998). Without entitlement to SSDI or SSI, alcoholics and addicts may also be unable to participate in the nation's major publicly-supported health care programs.

The federal Personal Responsibility and Work Opportunity Reconciliation Act (PRWORA) of 1996, known as "welfare reform," made massive changes in the federal Food Stamp Program (FSP) and the major state-run public assistance programs for poor families with children, now called the Temporary Assistance for Needy Families (TANF) program (DiNitto, 2000). For example, convicted drug felons are barred from TANF and FSP forever unless the state passes a law to opt out or modify this provision (see Adams, Onek, & Riker, 1998). Their children retain the right to benefits, but there is less help for the entire family. States can also test adult TANF recipients for drug use and penalize them if they test positive. Though few have resorted to "suspicionless" testing, some have adopted testing based on suspicion of use or other screening techniques, including self declaration (Carey, 1998). The federal Department of Housing and Urban Development's "one strike" policy means that public housing tenants can be evicted for drug use or related activities and, although declared unconstitutional by the 9th Circuit Court, in some communities or jurisdictions innocent individuals residing with drug users or sellers may be evicted as well ("Court overturns . . . ," 2001).

Under the current federal Higher Education Act, students with adult drug convictions are denied federal financial aid to attend college for varying lengths of time (see "Injustice 101 . . . ," 2001). Public school districts have used "zero tolerance" policies to suspend or expel children who are found with banned substances (see "Schools reconsider . . . ," 2001). Some public school districts have mandated drug testing of all high school students. Penalties for refusing to be tested include bans on participating in extracurricular activities. The American Academy of Pediatrics believes that without strong medical or legal justification, involuntary testing is not appropriate for young people while the Academy believes that there is cause for concern about psychoactive drug use, the response should be referral to a qualified professional (Committee on Substance Abuse, 1996, p. 305). Given constitutional challenges, such as unreasonable searches, the U.S. Supreme Court will take up the issue of drug testing of school children ("U.S. Supreme Court to advise . . . ," 2001).

Though the benefits of widespread drug testing of employees are questionable, it has become an increasingly common practice (Normand, Lempert, & O'Brien, 1994). Drug testing in the workplace usually fails to address the abuse of alcohol–the substance most often associated with job performance problems.

The war on drugs has been branded as discriminatory and racist. Though the prosecution of women for fetal endangerment does not hold up well under judicial scrutiny, women, particularly poor women, have been arrested or incarcerated for drug use while pregnant (see Paltrow, Cohen, & Carey, 2000). There are also concerns that children's protective services are not addressing parental alcohol and other drug use appropriately. Penalties for possession of crack cocaine, which is readily available in poor communities inhabited disproportionately by members of particular ethnic groups, are much harsher than penalties for possession of powdered cocaine, which is more expensive to obtain. African Americans have been hit hardest by this disparity (see United States Sentencing Commission, 1995, 1997).

Will the War Abate?

Conspicuously absent from the drug war are many aspects of harm reduction–in particular, needle exchange. Although the federal Department of Health and Human Services (DHHS) has acknowledged the benefits of needle exchange (e.g., reduced HIV transmission and no encouragement of injection drug use), it has refused to fund such programs, saying that the decision should be left to local communities ("Research shows . . . ," 1998). Provision of clean syringes to drug addicts remains illegal in most jurisdictions. Individuals who operate such programs risk arrest, though law enforcement may not interfere with their efforts.

There is some evidence that the drug war may be abating. For example, the number of community drug courts, which offer treatment in lieu of prosecution to first-time and low-level, non-violent drug offenders, is increasing (ONDCP, 2001). California voters recently approved Proposition 36; it diverts all first- and second-time non-violent drug possession offenders to treatment rather than incarceration (Vallianatos, 2001).

ACCESS TO CHEMICAL DEPENDENCY TREATMENT

The U.S. spends a greater percentage of its gross domestic product on health care than all other developed countries, yet fewer Americans are covered by health insurance than citizens of these other countries (Organization for Economic Cooperation and Development [OECD], 2001). Those with health insurance usually have some coverage for alcohol and drug dependence treatment.

In the U.S., private practitioners provide most health care, and health insurance is generally obtained through one's employer (for an overview of U.S. health care policy, see DiNitto, 2000). There are two major publicly-supported health insurance programs, designed largely to cover those outside the workforce. Medicare, a federally administered social insurance program (employers and employees pay into the program during the employee's working years), covers virtually all those aged 65 or older. Medicaid, a public assistance program financed jointly by the federal government and the states, covers poor Americans who must also meet other eligibility criteria, such as being under age 18, being pregnant, or having a disability (other than alcohol or drug dependence) that prevents gainful employment. Medicaid and Medicare generally cover chemical dependency treatment (see Coffey et al., 2001); however, most poor Americans do not qualify for Medicaid because income and assets limitations are so stringent, or because they do not meet other eligibility criteria. Many physicians (and other practitioners) accept Medicare's federally-established reimbursement rates, but most do not accept Medicaid because state-determined reimbursement rates are so low. The type and extent of Medicaid coverage for chemical dependency (and many other services) varies considerably by state (see McNeece & DiNitto, 1998).

Fourteen percent of Americans did not have any public or private health insurance coverage in 2000 (U.S. Bureau of the Census, 2001), and therefore, had no coverage for chemical dependency treatment. Many others were not insured during part of the year. Many of the uninsured are the "working poor." Their employers do not provide health insurance or they are self-employed, they do not meet Medicaid requirements, and they cannot afford to purchase health insurance on their own. Unless those who are uninsured and need chemical dependency treatment can afford to pay for private care out-of-pocket, or unless they rely solely on no-cost services like Alcoholics Anonymous (AA), their alternative is to utilize over-subscribed public or private not-for-profit community-based alcohol and drug treatment programs. These programs are supported through a variety of means, such as public and private insurance programs; state, federal, and private grants and contracts; city and county governments; donations; and modest fees that clients may be able to pay. Community-based treatment programs may be free-standing alcohol and drug treatment agencies, or they may be operated by agencies like community mental health centers. Some patients are also treated in state mental hospitals, though the trend has been to use these hospitals only when the individual has a severe mental illness in addition to a diagnosis of alcohol or drug dependency.

Access to chemical dependency treatment is a problem for many Americans who need assistance (CSAT, 2000). It is also an issue for social workers who must work diligently to help clients with few resources find treatment slots. Though community-based services can be of high quality, there are often waiting lists for detoxification, inpatient, or residential treatment beds, and for outpatient services as well. Judges and other players in the criminal justice system may require their charges to participate in chemical dependency treatment even when there is no inpatient or outpatient treatment slot to be had. Social workers often try to get their clients in ahead of the queue by expounding on the gravity of their client's situation.

MANAGING CHEMICAL DEPENDENCY TREATMENT

The recent phenomenon called "managed care" has had a significant impact on health care in the United States in the public, private-not-for-profit, and private-for-profit sectors (see McNeece & DiNitto, 1998). Managed care organizations (MCOs) control health care costs through utilization review (monitoring patients' health care use) and restricting or limiting access to health care services or health care providers (see DiNitto, 2000). The restrictions or limitations may mean that patients cannot access health care services, including mental health and chemical dependency treatment, at will, but must be referred by their primary health care physician (unless they are willing to pay the costs themselves). Patients may also be required to use designated service providers, or their insurer will reimburse at higher rates when designated providers are used. Providers, including social workers, spend a good deal of time negotiating patients' or clients' care with MCOs, often begging for inpatient rather than outpatient treatment, a few more days in detoxification, or a few more sessions of outpatient therapy (McNeece & DiNitto, 1998). Providers also spend a good deal of time negotiating their contracts with MCOs and dealing with record-keeping and billing technology. Franklin (2001) calls this "coming to terms with the business of direct practice" (p. 235). MCOs contract with treatment providers of their choice. Social workers and other providers who get into too many conflicts with the MCO over treatment plans and reimbursement rates may find their contracts terminated. MCOs rely heavily on empirical evidence of treatment efficacy in approving requests for services, and a common complaint is that administrators control health care decisions more than treatment providers and patients.

Managed care arose due to spiraling health care costs. Before managed care, inpatient chemical dependency treatment, including expensive hospital stays, was the norm for patients whose insurance covered it (McNeece & DiNitto, 1998). In fact, inpatient care was often the only service covered by insurance. Over the years, studies have shown that for many individuals, inpatient alcoholism treatment is no more effective than outpatient treatment (NIAAA, 2000). Outpatient care is also less costly, and managed care has caused it to be used more widely.

The *Diagnostic and Statistical Manual of Mental Disorders (DSM)*, published by the American Psychiatric Association (2000), has a substantial influence on the treatment of substance use disorders in the U.S. The *DSM* classifications of these disorders are *abuse* and *dependence*. Treatment is generally provided for the diagnosis of dependence. There is little more than brief intervention for substance abuse. In order to ensure that their patients or clients qualify for treatment and to ensure payment for treatment rendered, chemical dependency professionals have to be very familiar with *DSM* criteria.

A Long Way from Parity

The federal Mental Health Parity Act of 1996 was designed to improve access to mental health care, but does not include services for substance use disorders. Many states limit parity to serious mental ill-ness, and few include chemical dependency services (see Sing, Hill, Smolkin, & Heiser, 1998). Whether required to do so or not, many health insurers (including managed care plans) offer coverage for chemi-cal dependency, though this coverage is often more limited than it is for mental health services. For example, chemical dependency services may be limited to 20 sessions of outpatient counseling a year and to 30 to 60 days of inpatient care, and this care may be further limited by *medical ne-cessity*, a term open to interpretation (Iglehart, 1996; Pomerantz, 1996).

Most large employers "carve out" their "behavioral health" (mental health and chemical dependency) coverage, meaning that they contract with specialized organizations to administer these services (Iglehart, 1996). Chemical dependency services may also be carved out from mental health services. Those in the chemical dependency field worry that their services will remain a stepchild, not only to health services, but to mental health services as well. "Carve outs" raise questions about whether separate providers can serve clients in a holistic fashion.

A major study of employer-provided health benefits in the U.S. shows that from 1988 to 1998, the value of health care benefits for the treatment of substance use disorders declined from 0.7% to 0.2% of the plans' overall value (Hay Group, 1998). The American Society of Addiction Medicine (1999) reports "a drastic reduction in frequency and duration of inpatient hospitalization [for people with substance use disorders], even for many patients who require this level of treat-ment intensity," with managed care plans authorizing inpatient treat-ment only in life-threatening cases. A review of studies indicated that outpatient care has not substituted for inpatient care in a number of cases, or that insurers were covering detoxification as the only inpa-tient treatment service (Mechanic, Schlesinger, & McAlpine, 1995), despite the knowledge that "detox" alone is generally ineffective in promoting recovery (see, for example, Gerstein & Harwood, 1990; NIDA, 1999).

Shulman (1994) adds that a patient may be required to "fail" at outpa-tient treatment before inpatient care is authorized, patients who do not use the maximum number of inpatient treatment days allotted for a treatment episode may not be allowed to use the unused days later, and residential or supported living may not be covered, resulting in use of hospital care when intensive outpatient care with supported living ar-rangements may be at least as helpful and less costly. Only 56% of MCOs cover outpatient methadone treatment ("Managed care . . . ," 2000). After studying treatment services provided to more than 7,000 alcoholics and drug addicts in the U.S., Miller and Hoffman (1995) concluded that many health care plans do not provide a continuum of care for these individuals; instead, most health care providers use an acute care model for a problem that is chronic for many individuals.

Mental health and chemical dependency treatment advocates continue to call for insurance benefits that are on par with other health care services. Estimates are that mental health parity would result in an average premium increase of 3.4% and that substance abuse coverage would add only 0.2% (Sing et al., 1998). In the U.S., special interest groups drive policy decisions (DiNitto, 2000). AA, the largest organization of recovering alcoholics in the world, does not engage in political activities, and no group has wielded sufficient political clout to improve chemical dependency treatment coverage. Barring a cure for chemical dependency, it is unlikely that much more will be accomplished in the insurance arena without greater political organization. It is up to employers who negotiate with health insurance organizations over the extent of mental health and chemical dependency benefits they can afford to provide for their employees.

TRANSFERRING ADVANCEMENTS IN RESEARCH AND TREATMENT TECHNOLOGY

Thanks to research, knowledge of alcohol and other drug problems and their remedies continues to grow. The U.S. government is the largest funder of alcohol and drug abuse prevention and treatment research in the world. The major conduit for this funding is the Department of Health and Human Services, which contains the National Institutes of Health (NIH) and the Substance Abuse and Mental Health Services Administration (SAMHSA). NIH is the home of the National Institute on Alcohol Abuse and Alcoholism (NIAAA) and the National Institute on Drug Abuse (NIDA), which focus mainly on research. Many state governments and private foundations also support alcohol and drug research. The current emphasis is not only in generating research but seeing that it gets translated into practice. SAMHSA houses the Center for Substance Abuse Treatment (CSAT) and Center for Substance Abuse Prevention (CSAP); both focus on applying knowledge to practice.

Of great interest to many in the chemical dependency treatment field are some of NIAAA's recent, major studies, including the Collaborative Study on the Genetics of Alcoholism (COGA), Project MATCH, and Project COMBINE. COGA is a pedigree study conducted by six research centers that are exploring the genetic vulnerability to alcoholism. Among the findings of COGA researchers are evidence of susceptibility loci for alcohol dependence on chromosomes 1, 2, and 7, and a possible protective locus on chromosome 4 (Reich, Edenberg, Goate, Rice, Van Eerdewegh et al., 1998). As exciting as this line of research is, social workers and others are concerned about its ethical implications, such as how information about the *potential* for alcohol and other drug addiction will be utilized.

Matching and Combining

More relevant to social workers' and other treatment providers' current work is Project MATCH. The study's hypothesis was that alcoholic clients would have better treatment results if they were matched to treatment based on their needs and characteristics (such as gender and cognitive impairment) as opposed to a "one treatment fits all" approach. This 5-year, $25 million study, begun in 1989, was a large-scale (n = 1,700), multi-site trial of three highly structured, short-term (either 4 or 12 sessions), psychosocial treatments (Twelve-Step Facilitation, Motivational Enhancement Therapy, and Cognitive-Behavioral Therapy) (Project MATCH Study Group, 1997). Since the need for treatment in the U.S. far outstrips treatment supply, it is tempting to consider short-term treatment approaches, especially treatments like these which practitioners can readily incorporate in their work and which also appeal to managed care providers. Some clients received the time-limited treatments as aftercare following inpatient or intensive day hospital treatment; others received it as outpatient treatment.

Except for cannabis, those also dependent on other drugs, whose multiple drug dependencies may be more difficult to overcome, were excluded from participation (not surprising since NIAAA rather than NIDA funded the study). In addition, there was no control group to determine how the alcoholic clients would have fared without any treatment. The research team found only four "matches" among the 21 variables studied (for example, clients in outpatient treatment who had low psychiatric severity drank on fewer days after Twelve-Step Facilitation than after Cognitive-Behavioral Therapy) (NIAAA, 2000). The most striking study finding was that *clients tended to improve regardless of which treatment they received.* The three treatments used in Project MATCH were produced in manual form to promote treatment fidelity in the study and transferability to practice. Of course, many clients treated by social workers and other practitioners require more than short-term interventions, and these standardized treatments must be adapted to suit the needs of the clientele.

Another addiction research topic of considerable interest in the U.S. is that of brain chemistry (see Erickson & Wilcox, 2001; NIAAA, 2000; Spencer, DiNitto & Straussner, 2002). Neurobiological research has resulted in the identification of neurotransmitters involved in drug actions and the testing of medications that may reduce cravings for alcohol and other drugs or otherwise promote more normal brain functioning among addicts. NIAAA recently launched Project COMBINE, which will study both psychosocial treatments and medications in a sample of over 1,300 clients (see Zweben, 2001). The psychosocial approaches are (1) Combined Behavioral Therapy (CBT), a moderate intensity treatment which is a blend of elements of the three treatments used in Project MATCH, and (2) Medication Management (MM), a brief treatment to encourage medication compliance along with abstinence. The medications being tested are naltrexone and acamprosate. Naltrexone, an opiate antagonist, has been used for some time in treating narcotic addicts. Naltrexone is also thought to reduce the craving for alcohol or the pleasurable effects of drinking. Acamprosate may have similar benefits, but it affects different biochemical pathways than naltrexone. Although this mechanism is not entirely clear, the drug is thought to restore normal activity in the glutamate and gamma-aminobutyric acid systems (see NIAAA, 2000). Since their mechanisms of action differ, the drugs will be administered alone and in combination to those receiving either CBT or MM to determine whether treatment outcomes are affected. Though approved for use in alcoholism treatment in the U.S., naltrexone has been utilized very little, perhaps due to factors such as cost or the idea that addictions should not be treated with drugs, even if the drugs are non-addictive (see, for example, Rawson, McCann, Hasson, & Ling, 2000). Acamprosate is used in many countries (NIAAA, 2000) but has not been approved for use in the U.S., where the process for approving new drugs can move slowly.

As we begin to think of alcohol and other drug dependence as brain diseases, chemical dependency treatment providers, most of whom do not have a medical background, are seeking more knowledge about the workings of the brain and the neurobiology of addiction. We are also recognizing the fallacy of mind-body dualism (Johnson, 2001). The biopsychosocial approach can no longer be conceived of as three separate entities with doctors focusing on the biological aspects, psychologists on the psychological aspects, and social workers on the socioenvironmental aspects. In fact, we are coming to believe that psychosocial treatments change brain chemistry by affecting emotional learning (Erickson & Wilcox, 2001). The idea that social workers might have a role to play in helping clients alter their brain chemistry, as well as their behavior, through psychosocial treatments is fascinating (Spence et al., 2002).

Bridging the Research-Treatment Gap

Countless studies in addition to COGA, MATCH, and COMBINE are providing new knowledge, but the concern is that research knowledge does not get readily translated into improved clinical practice. As said in the Paul Newman movie *Cool Hand Luke*, there has been "a failure to communicate." A blueprint for transferring research findings to practice is *Bridging the Gap Between Practice and Research: Forging Partnerships with Community-Based Drug and Alcohol Treatment* (Lamb, Greenlick, and McCarty, 1998). The Clinical Trials Network (CTN), a NIDA project established in 1999, is an attempt to increase knowledge exchange between researchers and addiction practitioners. Among the interventions being tested through the CTN are the use of Motivational Interviewing ("Clinical Trials Network," January, 2001) and the use of buprenorphine in treating opiate addiction ("Clinical Trials Network," February, 2001).

Other efforts to bridge the gap are the 13 CSAT-funded regional Addiction Technology Transfer Centers (ATTCs) and the national ATTC office, which work to increase practitioners' "access to state-of-the-art research and education" (see www.nattc.org). Many social workers are involved in the ATTCs. Another CSAT initiative, Practice/Research Collaboratives (PRCs), are designed to increase communication among treatment providers, researchers, policymakers, consumers, and other stakeholders. PRCs emphasize improved substance abuse prevention and treatment by implementing and evaluating evidence-based approaches in community settings. Social workers are taking a more prominent role in NIAAA-, NIDA-, and SAMHSA-funded research. NIDA has begun a new initiative called Social Work Research Development Programs to provide the infrastructure that schools of social work need in order to develop strong research proposals in the highly competitive federal funding arena (see nida.nih.gov).

Bridging the Research-Prevention Gap

Preventing as well as treating substance abuse is a major goal of U.S. drug policy. The most popular prevention strategy has been the Drug Abuse Resistance Education (D.A.R.E.) program, which is delivered by police officers in school classrooms. Although this tremendously popular program, now two decades old, has reportedly been used in 75% of U.S. public school districts, studies indicate that it is apparently ineffective in preventing and reducing drug use, especially in the long run (see, for example, Lynam, Milich, Zimmerman, Novak, Logan, Martin et al., 1999; Ringwalt, Greene, Ennet, Iachan, Clayton, & Leukefeld, 1994; Sager, 2000). A primary suggestion has been to make the program more interactive (Ringwalt et al., 1994). A grant from the Robert Wood Johnson Foundation is being used to test a revised D.A.R.E. curriculum.

The Center for Substance Abuse Prevention has identified a number of prevention programs with demonstrated effectiveness (see www.samhsa. gov/centers/csap/csap.html). These model programs rely on a variety of strategies and target youth of various age groups. Among them are Gilbert Botvin's Life Skills Training, which targets children aged 10-14 and focuses on life skills, drug resistance skills, and social and self-management skills, and Karol Kumpfer's Strengthening Families program, which targets children aged 6-11 and their parents and uses therapeutic child play, parent training, and support services.

KEEPING THE FAITH: AA, SPIRITUALITY, AND RELIGION

Alcoholics Anonymous (AA) (2000) continues to exert a tremendous influence on the way alcohol problems are addressed in the U.S. An estimated 60% of its two million members reside in the U.S. Though difficult to assess scientifically, AA is widely perceived as the most effective approach to recovery from alcoholism. There is no question that many individuals attribute their recovery to AA or its offshoots, such as Narcotics Anonymous. Though the word "God" is used in several of the 12 steps, and the Lord's Prayer is recited at meetings, AA (1952) describes itself as a "spiritual," not a "religious" program. AA (1952) also reports that agnostics and atheists have recovered through the program, and those of various religious persuasions have adapted the program to suit their needs (see, for example, Master, 1989).

The criminal justice system often mandates that probationers and parolees participate in AA, Narcotics Anonymous, or similar 12-step programs, regardless of individuals' spiritual or religious beliefs. A 1996 ruling by New York's highest court, which challenged the practice because AA participation constitutes religious activity (see "NY Court . . . ," 1996), seems to have had little effect. The abstinence-based approach of AA permeates the services offered by treatment programs in the U.S. AA is self-supporting through the contributions of its own members, it takes no political positions, and it is not affiliated with other programs, yet AA is so well respected that some treatment programs go so far as to say that they are based on AA principles.

Religious organizations play an important part in chemical dependency rehabilitation in the U.S. Prominent among them is the Salvation Army, which far exceeds any other charitable organization in the donations it receives (Lipman, 2000). The Salvation Army has had a long history of assisting alcoholics and addicts with its own combination of rehabilitation and religion (White, 1998).

Social workers in the U.S. have long worked for religiously-affiliated organizations such as Catholic Charities, Lutheran Social Services, and Jewish Community Services (see National Association of Social Workers [NASW], 2001). Social work education programs attract many students who are motivated by their religious (as well as political) convictions. Social workers are, however, not unanimous about the separation of religion from their professional roles. For example, the North American Association of Christians in Social Work "supports the integration of Christian faith and professional social work practice in the lives of its members" (www.nacsw.org).

Conservative religious groups are wielding considerable influence on U.S. politics. These groups have come to be known as the "religious right," and in social welfare circles they have adopted a philosophy called "compassionate conservatism" (see Olasky, 2000). In recent years, religiously affiliated organizations have been able to obtain public funds to provide social services as long as they do not use them for religious activities. In 1996, the religious right helped bring about the substantial overhaul of the country's public assistance system under the PRWORA. This overhaul contains a provision called "charitable choice" which expands faith-based groups' opportunities to receive public funding to provide social services in certain programs, including substance abuse treatment programs.

President George W. Bush's efforts to expand charitable choice provisions include establishing the White House Office of Faith-Based and Community Initiatives (see www.whitehouse.gov). In a country predicated on the separation of church and state, this effort is raising much discussion. The provision of government funds to religious organizations raises a specter that many find difficult to reconcile (see NASW, 2001). It raises concerns about funding religious activities, about what sects will qualify and how these decisions will be made, and about whether substance abuse and other social services will be provided by qualified individuals. Although some religious organizations want government funding, others worry that it could change their organizations in ways they might not desire. The effectiveness of religious-based substance abuse programs has not been well studied, but researchers are finding this an interesting new line of inquiry. Many would agree that recovery from chemical dependency involves some type of personal transformation, but the expansion of charitable choice could change chemical dependency treatment as we know it. The National Association of Social Workers (2001) has issued a position statement expressing its concern about President Bush's faith-based initiative.

SOCIAL WORK CREDENTIALING AND CHEMICAL DEPENDENCY TREATMENT

There are three levels of social work education in the U.S.: bachelor's, master's, and doctoral. The bachelor's and master's are called practice degrees. The Council on Social Work Education (CSWE) is the accrediting body for these education programs. There are approximately 420 accredited bachelor's programs and 140 accredited master's programs (see www.cswe.org). CSWE's Educational Policy and Accreditation Standards (EPAS) makes no mention of alcohol and other drug content (see www.cswe.org). Rationales for not requiring content in particular practice areas such as substance abuse are that the list is endless and programs should be free to select their own emphases.

Bachelor's level social work education programs prepare students for generalist practice. Bachelor's programs do not offer specializations in particular areas of social work practice per se, but many bachelor's and master's social work education programs offer one or more elective courses on alcohol and drug problems, and some master's programs offer concentrations or post-master's certificate programs in chemical dependency. Little systematic information is collected on the alcohol and drug content in social work education programs, though CSWE reports that in the fall of 1999, only 1.2% of master's degree students were enrolled in alcohol and drug problem concentrations, and 2.8% of master's students had field placements focused on alcohol and drug problems (Lennon, 2001). Students can often use the substance abuse courses and internships that social work education programs offer to pursue state certification or licensure as an alcohol or drug abuse counselor. Dual diagnoses courses, which recognize that many clients have mental or other disabilities in combination with substance use disorders that require integrated treatment, are also emerging.

Since the inception of social work as a profession in the U.S., social workers have assisted people who have alcohol and drug problems and their families (see Straussner, 2001). Social workers' education about chemical dependency has been enhanced by the emergence of social work texts in the field (see Abbot, 2000; McNeece & DiNitto, 1998; Straussner, 1993; Van Wormer, 1995); the *Journal of Social Work Practice in the Addictions*, the first social work journal in the field; and curriculum modules produced specifically for social workers by the National Association of Social Workers (CSAP, 1995). NIAAA is currently preparing a new set of modules on alcohol problems.

With 155,000 members, NASW is the largest membership organization of social workers in the world (see www.naswdc.org). In a recent survey of 2,000 randomly selected members, only 2% named addictions as their primary practice area ("72 Percent Work . . . ," 2001). However, 71% reported having "taken one or more actions in relation to clients with substance abuse disorders in the past year" (O'Neill, 2001, p. 10). Of the respondents, 81% report some preparation for work with clients who have substance use disorders, primarily continuing education workshops and clinical supervision. Only 38% report formal coursework. Eight percent of respondents had some type of substance abuse certification or licensure. Concern remains that the addictions knowledge of many social workers is insufficient (Flanzer, 2001).

NASW recently developed an Alcohol, Tobacco, and Other Drugs (ATOD) Section (see www.naswdc.org/sections/ATOD). NASW members may join the section for an annual fee that entitles them to receive the section's newsletter, *Issues of Substance*, and participate in the section's listserv called *ATODConnect*. There is also a newly established ATOD specialty certification for NASW members who have a master's degree in social work and hold either NASW's Academy of Certified Social Workers credential or Diplomate in Clinical Social Work credential, or the highest level of clinical licensing available in their state of residence. They must also meet other requirements, including 3,000 hours of post-social work master's degree paid supervised social work experience.

Credentialing is an important aspect of professional practice in the U.S. Every state has some form of social work regulation (see www.naswdc.org) usually *licensure* or *certification (*see the website of the Association of Social Work Boards at www.aswb.org). Many other helping professionals are also licensed or certified, including addiction counselors. Candidates for addiction counselor certification or licensure must generally pass an exam and provide proof of education in the field (courses, conferences, or institutes attended) and supervised work or internship experience, but an associate's, bachelor's, or master's degree in the helping professions or any other field is generally not necessary. Though chemical dependency treatment has become more "professionalized," this type of credential continues to provide an entrée to employment in the field for many recovering individuals and other interested parties.

In addition to state social work certification or licensure, many social workers who practice in the chemical dependency field hold a state license or certification in alcohol and drug counseling, either because the state or their employer requires them to do so, or because they believe that the credential establishes their credibility in this specialty area. They may also hold other credentials such as a license in marriage and family therapy or a certification in employee assistance counseling, offered by states or national organizations. Each credentialing body prescribes its own code of ethics, and each credential generally has an annual or biennial renewal fee and continuing education requirements that take time and money to attend. NASW's new ATOD certification is voluntary. Social workers, whose incomes are usually modest, will undoubtedly be weighing whether they can afford the credential and factors such as its potential to enhance their employment status.

CONCLUSION

Countervailing forces influence the treatment and prevention of alcohol and drug problems in the U.S. On the one hand, significant amounts of treatment research are being produced, and more effort is being made to see that it translates into improved practice. On the other hand, managed care has limited treatment access and duration, and federal drug policy continues to emphasize law enforcement and interdiction over prevention and treatment. New forces, such as an increased emphasis on the role of religious organizations in recovery, are also coming to bear. There are some signs that Americans are rethinking the long and hard fought drug war, since a law enforcement approach without sufficient treatment opportunities has not borne its intended fruits. Social workers in all practice areas need more alcohol and drug education to see that appropriate policies are implemented and to improve their effectiveness in preventing alcohol and drug problems and responding to clients who have these problems.

REFERENCES

Abbott, A. (Ed.) (2000). *Alcohol, tobacco, and other drugs: Challenging myths, assessing theories, individualizing interventions.* Washington, DC: NASW Press.

Adams, R., Onek, D., & Riker, A. (1998). *Double jeopardy: An assessment of the felony drug provision of the welfare reform act.* San Francisco: The Justice Policy Institute. Retrieved from <www.cjcj.org/jpi/doublejep.html>.

Alcoholics Anonymous. (1952). *Forty-four questions and answers about the A.A. program of recovery from alcoholism.* New York City: Alcoholics Anonymous World Services.

Alcoholics Anonymous. (2000, January 1). *Alcoholics Anonymous 1998 Membership Survey.* New York City: Author. Retrieved from <www.alcoholics-anonymous.org>.

American Psychiatric Association. (2000). *Diagnostic and statistical manual of mental disorders, 4th ed., text revision.* Washington, DC: Author.

American Society of Addiction Medicine. (1999, April 28). *The impact of managed care on addiction treatment: A problem in need of a solution.* Chevy Chase, MD: Author. Retrieved from <www.asam.org/ppol/managedcare.htm>.

Carey, C. A. (1998). Crafting a challenge to the practice of drug testing welfare recipients: Federal welfare reform and state response as the most recent chapter in the war on drugs. *Buffalo Law Review, 46,* 281. Retrieved from <http: web.lexis-nexis.com/universe/printdoc>.

Center for Substance Abuse Prevention. (1995). *Curriculum modules on alcohol and other drug problems for schools of social work.* Rockville, MD: Substance Abuse and Mental Health Services Administration.

Center for Substance Abuse Treatment. (2000). *Changing the conversation, Improving substance abuse treatment: The national treatment plan initiative.* Rockville, MD: Substance Abuse and Mental Health Services Administration, Department of Health and Human Services.

Clinical Trials Network. (2001, January 16). *Addiction Exchange 3* (1), newsletter of the Mid-Atlantic Addiction Technology Transfer Center. Retrieved from <www.mid-attc.org>.

Clinical Trials Network, part 2. (2001, February 1). *Addiction Exchange, 3* (2), newsletter of the Mid-Atlantic Addiction Technology Transfer Center. Retrieved from <www.mid-attc.org>.

Coffey, R. M., Mark, T., King, E., Harwood, H., McKusick, D., Genuardi, J., Dilonardo, J., & Chalk, M. (2001). *National estimates of expenditures for substance abuse treat-*

ment, 1997. Rockville, MD: Substance Abuse and Mental Health Services Administration. Retrieved from <www.samhsa.gov/centers/csat/content/idbse/sa01ch1.asp>.

Committee on Substance Abuse, American Academy of Pediatrics. (1996). Testing for drugs of abuse in children and adolescents. *Pediatrics, 98,* 305-307. Retrieved from <http://web.lexis-nexis.com/universe/printdoc>.

Committee on Ways and Means, U.S. House of Representatives. (1998). *1998 green book: Background material and data on programs within the jurisdiction of the Committee on Ways and Means.* Washington, DC: U.S. Government Printing Office.

Conklin, M. (1997). Out in the cold: Washington shows addicts the door. *The Progressive, 61* (3), 25-27.

Court overturns HUD's 'one strike' drug policy. (2001, January 26). Boston: *News Summary.* Boston University School of Public Health. Retrieved from <www.jointogether.org>.

de Miranda, J. (1990, August). The common ground: Alcoholism, addiction and disability. *Addiction and Recovery,* pp. 42-45.

DiNitto, D. M. (2000). *Social welfare: Politics and public policy.* Boston: Allyn and Bacon.

Erickson, C. K., & Wilcox, R. E. (2001). Neurobiological causes of addiction. *Journal of Social Work Practice in the Addictions, 1* (3), 7-23.

Flanzer, J. (2001, March). From the Chair . . . *Issues of Substance* (newsletter of the Alcohol, Tobacco, and Other Drug Section of the National Association of Social Workers), *6* (1), 2 & 7.

Franklin, C. (2001). Coming to terms with the business of direct practice social work. *Research on Social Work Practice, 11,* 235-244.

Gerstein, D. R., & Harwood, H J. (Eds.). (1990). *Treating Drug Problems,* Vol. 1. Washington, DC: National Academy Press.

Gray, M. (1998). *Drug crazy: How we got into this mess and how we can get out.* New York: Random House.

Hay Group. (1998). *Employer health care dollars spend on addiction treatment.* Chevy Chase, MD: American Society of Addiction Medicine. Retrieved from <http://www. asam.org/pressrel/hay.htm>.

Iglehart, J. K. (1996). Managed care and mental health. *The New England Journal of Medicine, 334* (2), 131-135.

Injustice 101: Government "Higher Education Act" denies financial aid to students with drug convictions. (2001, October 8). New York City: American Civil Liberties Union. Retrieved from <www.aclu.org>.

Johnson, H. C. (2001). Neuroscience in social work practice and education. *Journal of Social Work Practice in the Addictions, 1* (3) 81-102.

Lamb, S., Greenlick, M. R., & McCarty, D. (Eds.). (1998). *Bridging the gap between practice and research: Forging partnerships with community-based drug and alcohol treatment.* Washington, DC: Institute of Medicine, National Academy Press.

Lennon, T. M. (2001). *Statistics on social work education in the United States: 1999.* Alexandria, VA: Council on Social Work Education.

Lipman, H. (2001, November 2). Top charities see donations surge again. *The Chronicle of Philanthropy,* pp. 1 & 40.

Lynam, D. R., Milich, R., Zimmerman, R., Novak, S. P., Logan, T. K., Martin, C., Leukefeld, C., & Clayton, R. (1999). Project DARE: No effects at 10-year follow-up. *Journal of Consulting and Clinical Psychology, 67,* 590-593.

Managed care not stepping up to cover methadone treatment. (2000, April 24). *Alcoholism & Drug Abuse Weekly,* p. 1.

Master, L. (1989). Jewish experience of Alcoholics Anonymous. *Smith College Studies in Social Work, 59,* 183-199.

McNeece, C. A., & DiNitto, D. M. (1998). *Chemical dependency: A systems approach,* 2nd ed. Boston: Allyn and Bacon.

Mechanic, D., Schlesinger, M., & McAlpine, D. D. (1995). Management of mental health and substance abuse services: State of the art and early results. *The Milbank Quarterly, 73* (1), 19-55.

Miller, N. S., & Hoffman, N. G. (1995). Addictions treatment outcomes. *Alcoholism Treatment Quarterly, 12* (2), 41-55.

National Association of Social Workers. (2001, July). NASW Position Statement: Faith Based Human Services Initiative. Washington, DC: NASW. Retrieved from <www.naswdc.org/advocacy/positions/faith.htm>.

National Institute on Alcohol Abuse and Alcoholism. (2000). *Tenth special report to the U.S. Congress on alcohol and health.* Rockville, MD: U.S. Department of Health and Human Services.

National Institute on Drug Abuse. (1999). *Principles of drug addiction treatment: A research-based guide.* Bethesda, MD: U.S. Department of Health and Human Services.

NY Court Lets Inmate Refuse Alcohol Program. (1996, June 12). New York City: American Civil Liberties Union. Retrieved from <www.aclu.org>.

Normand, J., Lempert, R. O., & O'Brien, C. P. (Eds.). (1994). *Under the influence? Drugs and the American workforce.* Washington, DC: National Academy Press.

Office of National Drug Control Policy. (1998). *The national drug control strategy, 1998.* Washington, DC: Executive Office of the President. Retrieved from <www.whitehousedrugpolicy.gov/publications/policy/98ndcs/contents.html>.

Office of National Drug Control Policy. (1999). *The national drug control strategy, 1999: Budget summary.* Washington, DC: Executive Office of the President.

Office of National Drug Control Policy. (2001). *The national drug control strategy: 2001 Annual Report.* Washington, DC: Executive Office of the President. Retrieved from <www.whitehousedrugpolicy.gov/publications/policy/ndcs01/strategy2001.pdf>.

Olasky, M. N. (2000). *Compassionate conservatism: What it is, what it does, and how it can transform America.* New York: Free Press.

O'Neill, J. V. (2001, January). Expertise in addictions said crucial. *NASW News* (newsletter of the National Association of Social Workers), p. 10.

Organization for Economic Cooperation and Development. (2001). *OECD health data 2001: A comparative analysis of 30 countries.* Paris: OECD. Retrieved from <www.oecd.org>.

Paltrow, L. M., Cohen, D. S., & Carey, C. A. (2000, October). *Governmental responses to pregnant women who use alcohol or other drugs: Year 2000 overview–an analysis.* Women's Law Project and National Advocates for Pregnant Women. Retrieved from <lindesmith.org/lindesmith/library/NAPWanalysis2.html>.

Pew Research Center. (2001). *74% say drug war being lost; interdiction and incarceration still top remedies.* Retrieved from <*www.people-press.org /drugs01que.htm*>.

Pomerantz, J. M. (1996). Letter to the editor. *The New England Journal of Medicine, 335* (1), 57.

Program on Employment and Disability. (2001). *Employing and accommodating individuals with histories of alcohol or drug abuse.* Ithaca, NY: Cornell University School of Industrial and Labor Relations.

Project MATCH Study Group. (1997). Matching alcoholism treatment to client heterogeneity: Project MATCH posttreatment drinking outcomes. *Journal of Studies on Alcohol, 58,* 7-29.

Rawson, R. A., McCann, M. J., Hasson, A. J., & Ling, W. (2000). Addiction pharmacotherapy 2000: New options, new challenges. *Journal of Psychoactive Drugs, 32,* 371-378.

Reich, T., Edenberg, H. J., Goate, A., Williams, J. T., Rice, J. P., Van Eerdewegh, P. et al. (1998). Genome-wide search for genes affecting the risk for alcohol dependence. *American Journal of Medical Genetics, 81,* 207-215.

Research shows needle exchange programs reduce HIV infections without increasing drug use. (1998, April 20). Washington, DC: U.S. Department of Health and Human Services press release. Retrieved from <www.hhs.gov/news/press/ 1998pres/980420a.html>.

Ringwalt, C. L., Greene, J. M., Ennett, S. T., Iachan, R., Clayton, R. R., & Leukefeld, C. G. (1994). *Past and future directions of the D.A.R.E. program: An evaluation review.* Research Triangle Park, NC: Research Triangle Institute.

Sager, R. H. (2000). Teach them well: Drug talk that fails. *National Review, 52* (8), 30-31.

Schools reconsider zero-tolerance policies. (2001, February 12). *News Summary.* Boston: Join Together, Boston University School of Public Health. Retrieved from <www.jointogether.org>.

72 percent work for private organizations. (2001, January). *NASW News* (newsletter of the National Association of Social Workers), p. 8.

Shulman, G. D. (1994, May-June). Costs: Don't blame them all on providers! *Behavioral Health Management,* 63-65.

Sing, M., Hill, S., Smolkin, S., & Heiser, N. (1998). *The costs and effects of parity for mental health and substance abuse insurance benefits.* Rockville, MD: Substance Abuse and Mental Health Services Administration. Retrieved <www.mentalhealth.org>.

Spencer, R.T., DiNitto, D. M. & Straussner, S.L.A (Eds) (2002). *Neurobiology of Addictions: Implications for Clinical Practice.* New York: The Haworth Press, Inc.

Straussner, S. L. A. (2001). The role of social workers in the treatment of addictions: A brief history. *Journal of Social Work Practice in the Addictions, 1* (1), 3-9.

Straussner, S. L. A. (Ed.). (1993). *Clinical social work with substance-abusing clients.* New York: Guilford.

U.S. Bureau of the Census. (2001, September 20). Health insurance coverage: 2000. Retrieved from <www.census.gov/hhes/hlthins/hlthin00/hlt00asc.html>.

United States Sentencing Commission. (1995). *Cocaine and federal sentencing policy.* Washington, DC: Author. Retrieved from <www.ussc.gov/crack/exec.htm>.

United States Sentencing Commission. (1997). *Cocaine and federal sentencing policy.* Washington, DC: Author. Retrieved from <www.ussc.gov/newcrack.pdf>.

U.S. Supreme Court to advise schools on drug testing. (2001, November 9). *News Summary.* Boston: Join Together, Boston University School of Public Health. Retrieved from <www.jointogether.org>.

Vallianatos, C. (2001, March). Voters approve drug-treatment plan. *NASW News* (newsletter of the National Association of Social Workers), p. 12.

Van Wormer, K. (1995). *Alcoholism treatment: A social work perspective.* Chicago: Nelson-Hall.

White, W. W. (1998). *Slaying the dragon: The history of addiction treatment and recovery in America.* Bloomington, IL: Chestnut Health Systems.

Zweben, A. (2001). Integrating pharmacotherapy and psychosocial interventions in the treatment of individuals with alcohol problems. *Journal of Social Work Practice in the Addictions, 1*(3).

Addiction Problems, Addiction Services, and Social Work in the Republic of Ireland

Shane Butler

SUMMARY. The aim of this paper is to review policy and practice in relation to the management of alcohol and drug problems in Ireland, with a specific focus on the role of professional social work. There is a high prevalence of alcohol and drug problems in the caseloads of social workers that work within the statutory childcare and criminal justice services. Professional social work in Ireland is of comparatively recent origin and there are few social workers employed in specialist addiction posts or settings in Ireland. The profession as a whole, moreover, has not actively lobbied for a greater role in specialist services. While formal social policy on addictions has shifted in recent decades towards broad public health strategies, which reflect a pragmatic European perspective, the disease model from the United States of America continues to have popular appeal. *[Article copies available for a fee from The Haworth Document Delivery Service: 1-800-HAWORTH. E-mail address: <getinfo@haworthpressinc.com> Website: <http://www.HaworthPress.com> © 2002 by The Haworth Press, Inc. All rights reserved.]*

KEYWORDS. Drug and alcohol policy in Ireland, social work education, childcare, criminal justice, specialist treatment, agency function

Shane Butler, MSocSc, CQSW, PhD, is Senior Lecturer at the Department of Social Studies, Trinity College, Dublin 2, Ireland (E-mail: sbutler@tcd.ie).

[Haworth co-indexing entry note]: "Addiction Problems, Addiction Services, and Social Work in the Republic of Ireland." Butler, Shane. Co-published simultaneously in *Journal of Social Work Practice in the Addictions* (The Haworth Social Work Practice Press, an imprint of The Haworth Press, Inc.) Vol. 2, No. 3/4, 2002, pp. 31-48; and: *International Aspects of Social Work Practice in the Addictions* (ed: Shulamith Lala Ashenberg Straussner, and Larry Harrison) The Haworth Social Work Practice Press, an imprint of The Haworth Press, Inc., 2002, pp. 31-48. Single or multiple copies of this article are available for a fee from The Haworth Document Delivery Service [1-800-HAWORTH, 9:00 a.m. - 5:00 p.m. (EST). E-mail address: getinfo@haworthpressinc.com].

INTRODUCTION

The Republic of Ireland, consisting geographically of about three quarters of the total island of Ireland, had its origins in the Anglo-Irish Treaty of 1921, at which time this portion of the country became self-governing while the remaining quarter, conventionally referred to as Northern Ireland, remained within the United Kingdom (UK). This partition of the country reflected religious as well as political differences, since the vast majority of those living in the Republic differed from those in Northern Ireland not just by virtue of their determination to secure political autonomy from Britain but also in that they were overwhelmingly Roman Catholic, while a majority of Northern Ireland residents were Protestant. The dominant influence of the Roman Catholic Church on social policy in the Republic has frequently been contentious, and it is noteworthy that until recently its influence on health and social service provision has been particularly strong (O'Dwyer, 2001).

Partition has always been a potential source of instability, and a protracted period of civil and paramilitary unrest within Northern Ireland, but with inevitable and profound negative implications for the Republic and for the wider UK, began in 1969 and continued unabated until the start of the current peace process in 1994. Despite such a turbulent history, this relatively new state has displayed remarkable political stability and an unambiguous commitment to democratic values and institutions (Coakley and Gallagher, 1999), and since 1973 the Republic (which will be referred to hereafter for the sake of simplicity as Ireland) has been a member of the European Union (EU). The Irish economy enjoyed unprecedented growth during the 1990s, and the current population of about 3.75 millions is the highest since the foundation of the state. This economic boom, referred to colloquially as the "Celtic Tiger," resulted in a reversal of the traditional pattern of emigration so that, for the first time ever, the state was compelled to adapt to a society that contained notable numbers of immigrants from a range of ethnic and religious backgrounds (Nolan, O'Connell and Whelan, 2000).

This brief historical and sociopolitical context may be of help in seeking to understand policy and service responses to alcohol and drug problems in Ireland. Because of its proximity to the UK and because it is almost entirely English-speaking, Ireland has obviously been heavily influenced in this, as in other spheres, by developments in Britain. On the other hand, because of historical ambivalence about its links with Britain, it has seemed at times as though Ireland is especially willing to look west to that other great English-speaking country, the United

States of America (USA), and to see this as an alternative and some-times more desirable source of influence in the shaping of public policy. And for the past thirty years, because of its ever-increasing integration into the EU, Ireland has been subject to much greater European policy influences than at any previous time.

Against this background, the aim of this paper is to review policy and practice in relation to the management of alcohol and drug problems in Ireland, with a specific focus on the role of professional social work in this sphere. To start with, some summary epidemiological data will be presented; this will be followed by a discussion of alcohol and drug pol-icy developments, which in turn will lead up to a fuller consideration of the way in which Irish social workers contribute to societal responses to addiction problems.

ALCOHOL AND DRUG PROBLEMS IN IRELAND

Alcohol consumption has long been a feature of Irish life, and sim-plistic and exaggerated stereotypes of excessive drinking amongst the Irish–particularly amongst the emigrant Irish in the USA (Stivers, 2000)–have had an international currency. While Roman Catholic tem-perance activities in Ireland date from the mid-nineteenth century (Malcolm, 1986), such activities have not been based upon the ideologi-cal rejection of alcohol which has characterized temperance in its Protestant manifestations in North America and in Scandinavian coun-tries (Levine, 1992). The *Pioneer Total Abstinence Association*, the temperance association that was founded in 1898 as an integral part of the Roman Catholic Church in Ireland, has continued to view absti-nence as a voluntary option to be undertaken by a minority of people for religious motives rather than as morally obligatory on all Catholics. In this tradition, alcohol is not seen as evil or problematic *per se* but rather as a Divine gift, albeit one which humanity may abuse and which may, accordingly, be implicated in a variety of personal and social problems. Since the 1960s, however, membership of this previously strong tem-perance movement has been on the decline (Ferriter, 1999) and, particu-larly during the 1990s and against the backdrop of the economic boom already referred to, there have been dramatic increases in alcohol con-sumption levels in this country. Hope (2001) has recently summarized data which reveal that:

- between 1989 and 1999, *per capita* alcohol consumption in Ireland increased by 41%, while nine EU countries showed a decrease, and three other EU countries showed only modest increases for the same period;
- in 1999, Ireland ranked third highest in the EU in terms of alcohol consumption, with Luxembourg occupying first place and Portugal second place in this league table;
- patterns of alcohol consumption vary across different age-groups, with younger drinkers tending to engage in more high-risk, binge-type drinking;
- in line with increased consumption levels, there are also indicators of increases in the incidence of alcohol-related problems, such as public order offenses and road traffic accidents, as well in a range of alcohol-related morbidity and mortality.

The use of illicit psychotropic drugs in Ireland is a relatively recent phenomenon, dating from the mid-1960s, and opiate use is of even more recent origin, dating only from 1980 (Butler, 1991). Prevalence cannot be estimated as readily or as reliably for illicit drugs as for alcohol, and international comparisons are therefore more complicated. However, the 1999 ESPAD (European School Survey Project on Alcohol and Other Drugs) study–which compares alcohol and drug use amongst 16-year-olds in 30 European countries–indicates a high lifetime prevalence of illicit drug use amongst Irish teenagers: the United Kingdom has the dubious distinction of being at the top of this list, with France and the Czech Republic sharing second place, and Ireland coming third (Hibell et al., 2000). The drugs that are most popular with Irish and other European teenagers are, in the main, those drugs traditionally categorized as "soft," with cannabis being a particular favorite. A consistent and obviously important epidemiological trend is the link between heroin use and social deprivation (O'Higgins, 1998; O'Higgins and Duff, 1997); heroin use in Ireland, has not been distributed randomly in geographic or socioeconomic terms but has clustered in areas of Dublin characterized by unemployment, poverty and communal demoralization. As might be expected, heroin use has contributed to a variety of related problems. A review of the epidemiology of AIDS in Ireland (O'Donnell, Cronin and Igoe, 2000) confirms that between 1983 and 1999 equipment sharing between injecting drug users was the most common mode of HIV transmission, accounting for 40% of cases of infection. There is also evidence of a strong, albeit complex, link between heroin use and crime; O'Mahony (1997), for instance, found in a survey of inmates in Mountjoy Prison–Ireland's largest prison–that 66% of his sample were heroin users.

ALCOHOL AND DRUG TREATMENT POLICIES IN IRELAND

Over the last half-century, treatment policy and service provisions for Irish people with alcohol or drug problems have undergone major change (see Butler, 1991; 1997; 1998; 2000, for more detailed discussion). From an ideological perspective, one of the features of this policy-making process has been the tension between two very different influences: the American influence which, crudely perhaps, may be characterized as favoring a disease model of addiction, with all that this implies, and a British or wider European influence which conceptualizes alcohol and drug problems in more disparate ways and which, in overall terms, is more pragmatic in defining acceptable outcomes to treatment and rehabilitation.

In relation to alcohol, between the late-1950s and the mid-1970s health policy makers in Ireland moved from an early and uncritical enthusiasm for the disease concept of alcoholism, to an almost total repudiation of it by the 1990s. An alternative public health or health promotional model, largely inspired by the World Health Organization (WHO) Europe, slowly gained favor, culminating in the publication of a national alcohol policy document in 1996 which did not even contain the word 'alcoholism' (*National Alcohol Policy-Ireland*, 1996). In this switch to a public health perspective, policy makers were expressing their conviction that the disease concept had been a bad import: one which had underestimated the risks inherent in alcohol consumption, while exaggerating the role of individual predisposition and also making extravagant claims for the efficacy of treatment.

However, while health policy makers at central government level may have become disillusioned with the validity and practicability of the idea of alcoholism as a discrete disease and have argued in a rational and evidence-based way for its replacement by a range of public health strategies, there has been little or no implementation of these strategies (Butler, 2001), and it would appear as though the Irish public is still wedded to the disease concept. Perhaps the clearest and most convincing evidence of the continuing popularity of the disease concept is to be found in the annual reports on the "activities" of the Irish psychiatric services, the most recent of which (Daly and Walsh, 2001) shows that during the year 2000 there were 4,517 psychiatric inpatient admissions–or 19% of all inpatient admissions for that year–for which the primary diagnosis was alcohol-related. This high proportion of alcohol-related psychiatric admissions reflects the persistent view of families, primary health care workers, the police, and problem drinkers themselves that the appropriate arena for the management of drinking problems is an inpatient psychiatric facility; this view has withstood policy attempts over almost twenty years to shift treatment away from inpatient facilities towards community-based and brief interventions. The notion that alcoholism is a definite and discrete disease, best treated by specialists within a structured treatment program and with abstinence as the only acceptable outcome, has been zealously promoted in Ireland by adherents of what is usually known as the Minnesota Model (Anderson, 1981), and who since the mid-1970s have succeeded in creating a network of treatment centers based on this model across the country. These Minnesota-style facilities have almost invariably been set up in the voluntary sector by Roman Catholic priests or nuns. Despite the fact that their fundamental philosophy is in contradiction of stated public policy in this field, they have been substantially funded from the public purse. The diffusion of the Minnesota Model to Ireland may be seen–drawing on the sociological work of Ritzer (1993)–as a *McDonaldization* of addiction treatment systems in this country. The resultant programs are homogenized, highly-structured, not always sensitive to or reflective of local culture, and not demonstrably effective, but for all that they are highly popular. Inherent in the disease concept as it has survived in Ireland is the assumption that specialist treatment personnel are preferable to generic or primary care workers, and an entirely new breed of specialist–the addiction counselor–has emerged. Despite some confusion as to its professional status, it has had considerable success in staking its claim in this arena.

From the mid-1960s till the mid-1980s, treatment programs for Irish people experiencing difficulties with illicit drugs were almost entirely based upon an abstinence model. The influence of the U.S. drug-free Therapeutic Community (TC) was strong, not just in treatment and rehabilitation circles, but also in the creation of some of the early education and prevention programs. As has been the case in other countries (Klingemann & Hunt, 1998), the major changes in Irish healthcare responses to drug use followed the advent of HIV/AIDS and the identification of needle-sharing amongst intravenous drug users as one of the major routes for the transmission of this virus. From the mid-1980s, healthcare services in Dublin have shifted incrementally, and with the minimum of publicity, towards the use of more pragmatic, harm reduction initiatives. Specific examples of harm reduction in the Irish system include the use of methadone maintenance and needle and syringe exchange schemes, as well as a restructuring of services in favor of decentralized clinics and outreach programs. In 1998, in what by American standards would seem a radical policy initiative, the role of family doctors in prescribing methadone to heroin addicts was legally institutionalized through what is colloquially known as the "Methadone Protocol."

Another significant policy change introduced in 1996, and which has continued to have ongoing high-level political support, resulted from the explicit acceptance of what the epidemiological data have consistently indicated, namely the link between serious drug problems and urban poverty and social exclusion. Under the rubric of *Local Drug Task Forces* (LDTFs), resources have been selectively targeted at those urban areas that have not benefited from the economic boom and which are identifiable as high risk for drug problems. Attempting to coordinate both preventive and rehabilitative activities at community level, LDTFs have been embedded within a new system of planning and management structures, the highest and most significant being a national Cabinet Committee on Social Inclusion. In early 2001, the Government also created a new community development initiative known as RAPID (Revitalizing Areas by Planning, Investment and Development). This initiative, while not drug-specific, is under the direction of the Minister responsible for national drug policy and is aimed at improving the physical infrastructure and the social and economic environment in low income urban areas. While it is too soon to reach conclusions about the impact that the LDTFs and RAPID are having on the prevalence of serious drug problems, these developments reflect an important philosophical shift in official drug policy, a shift which broadly speaking moves Ireland closer to those European countries–such as Germany and the Netherlands–which see urban regeneration as having a key role to play in the prevention of drug problems. The extent to which Irish drug policy has now shifted to an acceptance of the causal importance of structural, as opposed to individual factors, is reflected in the following remark of the Taoiseach (Prime Minister) at the launch of a new National Drugs Strategy: "If you think back just a short time, public drugs policy was very simple and summed up in the phrase 'just say no' . . . this approach ignored all sorts of basic issues fundamental to reducing drug misuse" (Ahern, 2001).

American influences on Irish drug policy and practice have obviously declined over the past decade. Since the establishment in 1993 of the European Monitoring Centre for Drugs and Drug Addiction (EMCDDA), an official EU body with specific responsibilities in this sphere, Irish research and drug policy formulation has become more "Europeanized."

It is against this policy background that we need to consider the precise role of Irish social work in both the prevention and the management of drug and alcohol problems. This will be looked at in the next two sections, and the relatively minor role that social work plays in the drug and alcohol sphere in Ireland will be highlighted. This minor role is explicable in terms of the newness of the profession in this country and the dominance of statutory agency function in day-to-day practice.

PROFESSIONAL SOCIAL WORK IN IRELAND

In Ireland, as in many other countries, social work as a secular profession evolved gradually from its roots in religious-based or philanthropic activities. The first major study of this historical evolution of professional social work in Ireland is that of Skehill (1999), in her introduction to which Kearney suggests that by international standards the professionalization of social work in this country was unusually slow and indirect. Acknowledging that most developments in this process took place in the half-century following the Second World War, she says that during this period "social work in Ireland developed not so much in leaps and bounds as in fits and starts" (Kearney, 1999, p. xii).

It was not until the late 1960s that Irish universities began to develop professional social work educational programs, and in 1971 a national professional organization, the Irish Association of Social Workers (IASW), was established. Until mid-1990s, university based social work programs were accredited by the British statutory body, the Central Council for Education and Training in Social Work (CCETSW). In 1995 an equivalent Irish state body, the National Social Work Qualifications Board (NSWQB) was established. Since its establishment, NSWQB policy on the style and content of professional social work education has deviated from British norms in favor of European models of social work education. At present, the minimum requirement for a professional qualification is a four-year undergraduate degree, but most Irish social workers now qualify having completed a three-year undergraduate degree in the social sciences, gained some work experience and then returned to university for a two-year master's program in social work. The role of the university in the professional socialization of social workers, with its implicit preference for *education* of reflective practitioners rather than *training* of technicians or welfare bureaucrats, seems more secure in Ireland than in Britain. It would be unwise, however, to regard this fact as being in any way indicative of how Irish social workers carry out their professional functions on a day-to-day basis. During the autumn of 1999, the NSWQB conducted the first ever national survey of social work posts (or positions) in Ireland (NSWQB, 2000), with *posts* being defined somewhat equivocally as Whole-Time Equivalent positions designated by human service agencies as social work posts. This survey revealed that:

- there were 1,390 social work posts in Ireland at this time and these were filled by 1, 528 practitioners; 85% of whom were professionally qualified;
- by international standards, the provision of social workers per head of population is unusually low in Ireland, being, for instance, only half that of the UK;
- the Department of Health and Children (a central government department) was the parent department for 83% of these posts;
- the Department of Justice, Equality and Law Reform was the parent department for 12% of these posts. These posts were in the criminal justice or corrections field within the Department's Probation and Welfare Service;
- 55% of the posts were concerned with child welfare: 39% were in child protection and welfare, 12% in specific adoption and fostering settings, and 4% in child psychiatric settings;
- only 8 posts (0.6% of the total) were described as being specifically in the addictions field;
- just 17.5 post (1.3% of the total) were in community work

Apart from an indeterminate, but probably small, number of social workers who are solely engaged in private practice as counselors or psychotherapists and whose activities were not captured by this survey, its data may be regarded as providing a comprehensive, detailed and reasonably up-to-date picture of Irish social work. The dominance of child welfare activities reflects the fact that, following the establishment of Ireland's regional health boards by the Health Act 1970, primary responsibility for child welfare was allocated to social workers employed by these boards. The enactment of the Child Care Act 1991 led to further strengthening of this role and to a major increase in the numbers of such social work posts. In summary, child protection and welfare has been the single arena within which there has been constant growth and expansion in the Irish social work labor market, just as it has been the single arena in which social work's claim to 'ownership' has been more or less uncontested. In a recent *British Journal of Social Work* commentary on social work in Ireland, Christie (2001) concluded that "Social work in Ireland has largely focused on children, adults as 'parents' and the 'family,' with other potential service users and ways of living being excluded from the professional 'gaze' "(pp.146-147).

While only 12% of social work posts were found to be within the criminal justice sector, it is to be expected that there will be major increases in this sector in line with an official 1999 review of the role of the Probation and Welfare Service, which recommended a much greater use of non-custodial sanctions for convicted offenders (*Final Report of the Expert Group on the Probation and Welfare Service,* 1999).

The findings of this survey also highlight the dominance of *agency function* in the professional lives of Irish social workers. By far the vast majority of social workers in this country are employed within statutory agencies where, it seems fair to assume, their daily activities are clearly delineated and constrained by laws, regulations and guidelines, and where the scope for independent judgement or professional discretion is quite restricted. Howe (1991), in an analytical review of British social work that would seem to be equally applicable to Ireland, suggests that power and influence on the shape of day-to-day social work practice may be regarded as being distributed between three types of professional: front-line practitioners themselves; social work administrators; and social work academics. He concludes that since most social workers are now employed in statutory agencies, such as those which are mandated to prevent the abuse or neglect of children, the lion's share of the power over practice decisions is currently enjoyed by administrators. Howe does not suggest that the other two groups are totally devoid of influence, nor does he see this situation as necessarily undesirable, but it is easy to see how social workers with expectations of a high degree of professional autonomy or the unfettered exercise of clinical judgement would find this situation frustrating.

It is worth noting the relative unimportance of community work as a source of employment for Irish social workers, and in this context to make it clear that social work has played little or no role in the emergence of policy and programs that link drug problems with social exclusion. Nonetheless, it would be naïve to interpret the finding of the 1999 survey that less than one per cent of Irish social workers are employed in posts which are designated as specialist addiction posts as proof that most social workers in this country are *not* regularly involved with clients who are experiencing drug or alcohol problems. Instead, it would seem more sensible to look for empirical evidence of the extent to which such problems manifest themselves in clients who are primarily categorized in some other way–as parents or as offenders, for example, since it is work with these two client groups which will mainly be considered here–and also to look at the way in which social workers who are not addiction specialists typically address these issues. In assessing the general adequacy of this non-specialist social work response to alcohol and drug problems, it is useful to draw again on Howe's framework by asking the following interlinking questions:

- how much direct work with substance misusing clients do front-line social workers actually do, or to what extent do they just assess and refer such clients on to specialist addiction agencies?
- how do social work managers, in agencies which are not specialist addiction agencies, interpret their role in dealing with such problems?
- what conceptual models of alcohol and drug problems are Irish social workers taught during the course of their professional socialization, and to what extent do these models fit with policy and practice in the agencies where they are subsequently employed?

ALCOHOL AND DRUG PROBLEMS IN CHILD CARE AND CRIMINAL JUSTICE SOCIAL WORK SETTINGS

If one starts with child protection and welfare and with Christie's (2001) previously cited contention that within Irish social work adults tend to be viewed primarily as *parents*, then one of the key questions to be addressed concerns the prevalence of alcohol and drug problems amongst those adults whose parenting has resulted in social work intervention. In a drinking culture–and there seems to be no disputing the fact that Ireland warrants such a description–it is to be expected that problem drinking by parents would regularly crop up as a contributory factor in cases of child neglect or abuse. Similarly, given the growth of opiate use and its associated problems since 1980, it is to be expected that parental opiate dependency would now be a prominent feature of child welfare and protection work in those urban areas where heroin use has become endemic.

Impressionistically, child protection and welfare work in Ireland is heavily burdened by parental addiction problems, but reliable statistics on this topic are not readily available. There has been little or no empirical research aimed at establishing the precise contribution of parental alcohol and drug misuse to child welfare problems, and official data-gathering on this subject–both at regional health board level and at national level–continues to be somewhat haphazard and methodologically suspect. Statistics from the Department of Health and Children (the central government department which formulates policy and funds childcare service provision) on the reasons why children are taken into the care of the state are produced irregularly and with little or no concern for methodological validity or reliability. For example, statistics on the 3,668 children who were in care on December 31, 1996, are broken down into nine specific categories that purport to explain the "principal reason for admission to care." Among the categories are the following– "parents unable to cope/parental illness," "physical abuse," "neglect," and "parents addicted to alcohol/drugs." In the case of each child in care, health boards (and presumably this task is carried out by health board social workers) were asked to select one category representing the principal reason for admission to care. Since most clients can be expected to experience multiple problems and since the categories are not discrete or mutually exclusive, this attribution of causality seems to be open to personal bias. For the country as a whole, 474 children (13%) were categorized as being in care because of parental addiction, but regional discrepancies in this category call into question its reliability. For example, within the Eastern Health Board region (which includes Dublin, the country's capital and most populous region) 18% of children were described as being in care for this reason; for the Mid-Western region this figure was 20%, but for the North-Western region *no* children were categorized in this way (Department of Health and Children, 2001).

Daly (1986), in what appears to be the only published study of the prevalence of drug and alcohol problems in the caseloads of child welfare social workers in Ireland, reviewed the caseloads of six social workers in the south inner-city of Dublin. At the time of this study, these social workers had a total active caseload of 112 families, of which 31 (28%) were identified as having drug or alcohol problems. Nineteen families had one or more adult members with an opiate problem, 17 had one or more adult member with an alcohol problem, and this included five families where alcohol and opiate problems coexisted. Nineteen (19) of the 31 families had children who had been taken into care, and between them these 19 families had 42 children in state care. During 1999, one predominantly rural health board carried out a detailed but unpublished survey of all the children in care in one of its community care areas. This health board found that parental addiction was the primary problem in the case of 41 out of 95 (43%) of children in care in that area. In this rural area the phrase "parental addiction" referred primarily to alcohol dependency, with illicit drug use being comparatively rare. This unpublished survey, which was made available to this author during the course of a consultancy project, will be referred to again later in this paper.

The centrality of drug and alcohol problems to the work of Irish Probation and Welfare Officers, on the other hand, is well documented both in official reports and empirical studies, and has been reviewed comprehensively in the *Final Report of the Expert Group on the Probation and Welfare Service* (1999). This report indicated that 56% of offenders in contact with the service during October 1998 were problem drug users. This official review is also valuable in that it explicitly identifies and discusses the various–and potentially conflicting–options open to the service in its management of these problems, a subject which will be returned to later in this paper.

SOCIAL WORK EDUCATION AND SOCIAL WORK PRACTICE

The NSWQB, the current statutory accreditation body for social work education and training in Ireland, has not laid down any guidelines governing the style or content of teaching on addictions in the social work curriculum, and it would appear that the curriculum development work initiated by CCETSW and directed by Larry Harrison of the University of Hull in the early 1990s (Harrison, 1992; 1993) still has a strong residual influence in the three Irish universities that currently offer professional social work programs. The main intention of this curriculum development work was not to introduce specific modules into social work qualifying programs that would equip students for specialist addiction posts but rather, drawing on the imaginative research of earlier British researchers (Cartwright, 1980; Shaw et al., 1978), to create a 'therapeutic commitment' to dealing with addictions amongst generic workers who invariably have a high prevalence of such problems in their caseloads. In keeping with this overall aim, Irish social work academics appear to favor models of practice, such as *motivational interviewing* and the *strengths perspective* (Loughran, 1994; Woods, 2000), which can be readily incorporated into non-specialist social work practice with addictions.

It appears, however, that this ambition on the part of Irish social work educators has had, at best, limited success, particularly in the field of Irish child care. The unpublished 1999 survey discussed above, which revealed that parental addiction was the major issue in relation to 43% of children in care in one area, highlighted the following difficulties:

- those social workers who had overall responsibility for managing child care did not really have any sense of therapeutic commitment to working directly with adults who had addiction problems, generally seeing this as a function of specialist addiction workers and services;

- those who specialized in addiction treatment, by and large, did not focus on parenting or on child care issues, despite the fact that many of their clients had young children who were directly affected by parental addiction;

- no formal or informal procedures or structures had been created to link or coordinate the work of these two forms of human service and, as a result, children of addicts rarely had their needs directly addressed so that they appeared to fall between two organizational stools.

What was disquieting about these research findings was that they suggested not merely that child care social workers failed to see themselves as credible therapists in relation to addictions, but also that they were not entirely confident in the role of case manager with cases like this. The findings of this survey are now being used to try to remedy this identified problem; and while it seems important that addiction specialists should be persuaded to take child care issues seriously, it is equally important that child care social workers should be assisted to challenge the mystique of specialist addiction work, to develop a critical appreciation of various models of addiction treatment, and to develop a stronger sense of their own professional adequacy in dealing with what are commonplace problems amongst their clients.

Further evidence that child care social workers appear to lack a routine sense of conviction about their capacity to assess and work effectively with addictions is to be found in the creation in 1997 of a specialist *Community (Social Work and Child Care) Drugs Service* (Eastern Health Board, 1997), which is aimed at improving social work with families where parents have serious opiate dependency. It could be argued that this project, which allowed social workers to work with relatively small case loads and to develop greater familiarity with opiate dependency, was an admirable initiative on the part of social work management, and its preliminary evaluation (Murphy and Hogan, 1999) was generally positive. However, given the prevalence of opiate dependency in Dublin and its negative impact on parenting, it could equally be argued that the knowledge, skills and general sense of adequacy which social workers displayed in this special project should be part of mainstream elements of all child care social work.

The Probation and Welfare Officers who work within the criminal justice system in Ireland have also labored under the same difficulties since there has never been organizational clarity as to what precisely their role should be in the management of offenders with drug or alcohol problems. Front-line Probation and Welfare Officers have tried with some success to create opportunities for themselves to expand their therapeutic work with these clients, and have also used their trade union to focus on addiction issues from a training and research perspective (Probation and Welfare Officers Branch of IMPACT Union, 1997). In addition, as mentioned above, addiction issues were explicitly discussed in a recent review document which went so far as to state that in relation to addictions there is no necessary conflict between the statutory, social control role of Probation and Welfare Officers, and their capacity to be therapeutic: "[T]he authority and capacity of Officers to invoke legal sanctions can add to rather than take from their therapeutic potential" (*Final Report of the Expert Group on the Probation and Welfare Service,* 1999, p. 74). This Expert Group did not consistently adhere to this point of view, however, and its final recommendations on this topic appear to favor the more traditional view, which is that Probation and Welfare Officers are best employed as case managers or agents of referral rather than as alcohol and drug therapists themselves.

CONCLUSION

Professional social work in Ireland is relatively new and job opportunities are primarily located in statutory agencies, particularly those that have responsibility for child welfare and protection or for dealing with offenders. Despite the prevalence of alcohol and drug-related problems in their caseloads, there has been little or no explicit debate on how addiction issues should be addressed in social work education. Irish social work educators appear to have been primarily influenced by British work on curriculum development in this area, emphasizing the importance of building up addictions knowledge and competence in mainstream or generic social work practitioners, rather than aiming to create a cadre of addiction experts. Generally, this academic perspective on addictions fits well with evolving social policy on alcohol and drug problems in Ireland, which has shifted from a somewhat narrow disease model and now conceptualizes these problems in broader public health terms. Within this public health perspective, the importance of socioeconomic and contextual factors is highlighted, and the capacity of non-specialist services and professionals to work effectively both at preventive and treatment levels is emphasized.

Paradoxically, popular opinion in Ireland continues to be heavily influenced by American disease model of addiction, which tend to favor addiction specialists, who are often located in residential treatment and rehabilitation services. Furthermore, Irish social work managers do not appear to have any definite vision of how their subordinates should deal with addictions and frequently go along with the popular view that referral to specialist addiction services is the best policy. It may also be, referring back to Howe's (1991) paper on what determines the nature of front-line practice, that most Irish social work managers simply find the idea of social workers as therapists or addiction counselors incompatible with bureaucratic requirements for processing large numbers of clients in a rational and systematic manner.

It is difficult to predict how professional social work in Ireland will resolve this dilemma and how it will evolve over the next few decades, but it seems reasonable to argue that one sign of professional maturity and self-confidence would be the emergence of educational and practice models that are *Irish* and appropriately reflective of the uniqueness of this culture and society. As the profession matures, it will perhaps no longer feel the necessity to cling grimly to its current base in child care, and it may feel confident to assert itself in relation to a number of other issues. Given the prevalence of alcohol and drug problems here, it would be a pity if a social work perspective was not developed and applied in this domain to a greater extent than has been the case thus far.

REFERENCES

Ahern, B. (2001). *Speech by the Taoiseach, Mr. Bertie Ahern TD at the launch of National Drugs Strategy, Thursday May 10, 2001, in the Press Centre, Government Buildings.*

Anderson, D.J. (1980). *Perspectives on Treatment: The Minnesota Experience.* Center City, MN: Hazelden.

Butler, S. (1991). Drug Problems and Drug Policies in Ireland: A quarter of a century reviewed. *Administration*, 39 (3), 210-233.

Butler, S. (1997). The War on Drugs: Reports from the Irish front. *Economic and Social Review*, 28 (2), 157-175.

Butler, S. (1998). Mental health social work and addictions in the Republic of Ireland. In Campbell, J. and Manktelow, R. (Eds.). *Mental Health Social Work in Ireland: Comparative issues in policy and practice* (pp.133-149). Aldershot: Ashgate.

Butler, S. (2000). A Tale of Two Sectors: A critical analysis of the proposal to establish drug courts in the Republic of Ireland. In Springer, A. and Uhl, A. (Eds.). *Illicit Drugs: Patterns of Use-Patterns of Response (Proceedings of the 10th Annual ESSD Conference on Drug Use and Drug Policy in Europe)* (pp. 47-58). Vienna: Studien Verlag.

Butler, S. (2001). The National Alcohol Policy and the Rhetoric of Health Promotion. *Irish Social Worker*, 19 (1), 4-7.

Cartwright, A. (1980). The Attitudes of Helping Agents Towards the Alcoholic Client: The influence of experience, support, training and self-esteem. *British Journal of Addiction*, 75 (4), 413-431.

Christie, A. (2001). Social Work in Ireland. *British Journal of Social Work*, 31 (1), 141-148.

Coakley, J. and Gallagher, M. (1999). *Politics in the Republic of Ireland* (3rd ed.). London: Routledge.

Daly, A., and Walsh, D. (2001). *Activities of Irish Psychiatric Services 2000*. Dublin: Health Research Board.

Daly, P. (1986). *Substance Abuse and Social Work Clients*. Dublin: Eastern Health Board.

Department of Health and Children (2001). *Survey of Children in Care of Health Boards at 31 December 1996*. Dublin: Department of Health and Children Website.

Ferriter, D. (1999). *A Nation of Extremes: The Pioneers in Twentieth-Century Ireland*. Dublin: Irish Academic Press.

Final Report of the Expert Group on the Probation and Welfare Service, (2001). Dublin: Stationery Office.

Harrison, L. (1992). Substance misuse and social work qualifying training in the British Isles: A survey of CQSW courses. *British Journal of Addiction*, 87 (4), 635-642.

Harrison, L. (Ed.). (1993). *Substance Misuse: Designing Social Work Training*. Central Council for Education and Training in Social Work and University of Hull.

Hibell, B., Andersson, B., Ahlstrom, S., Balakireva, O., Bjarnsason,T., Kokkevi, A. and Morgan, M. (2000). *The 1999 ESPAD Report: Alcohol and Other Drug Use Among Students in 30 European Countries*. Stockholm: The Swedish Council on Information on Alcohol and Other Drugs.

Hope, A. (2001). Alcohol Issues in Ireland, 1990-2000. Paper read at *Alcohol Policy–A Public Health Perspective* conference in Dublin Castle, November 20, 2001.

Howe, D. (1991). Knowledge, Power, and the Shape of Social Work Practice. In Davies, M. (ed.). *The Sociology of Social Work* (pp. 202-220). London: Routledge.

Kearney, N. (1999). Preface to Skehill, C. *The Nature of Social Work in Ireland: A historical perspective*. Lewiston, NY: Edwin Mellen Press.

Klingemann, H. and Hunt, G. (Eds.). (1998). *Drug Treatment Systems in an International Perspective: Drugs, Demons and Delinquents.* London: Sage.

Levine, H.G. (1992). Temperance Cultures: Concerns about alcohol problems in Nordic and English-speaking countries. In Lader, M., Edwards, G. and Drummond, D.C. (Eds.). *The Nature of Alcohol and Drug Related Problems.* (pp.15-36). London: Oxford University Press.

Loughran, H. (1994). Motivational Interviewing. *Irish Social Worker*, 12 (2), 14-15.

Malcolm, E. (1986). *'Ireland Sober, Ireland Free': Drink and Temperance in Nineteenth-Century Ireland.* Dublin: Gill and Macmillan.

Murphy, C. and Hogan, D. (1999). *Supporting Families Through Partnership: Eastern Health Board (Area 5) Community Drugs Service.* Dublin: Children's Research Centre, Trinity College Dublin.

National Alcohol Policy–Ireland (1996). Dublin: Stationery Office.

National Social Work Qualifications Board. (2000). *Social Work Posts in Ireland on 1 September 1999:A survey conducted by the NSWQB.* Dublin: NSWQB.

Nolan, B., O'Connor, P.J. and Whelan, T. (Eds.). (2000). *Bust to Boom? The Irish experience of growth and equality.* Dublin: Institute of Public Administration.

O'Donnell, K., Cronin, M. and Igoe, D. (2000). *Review of the Epidemiology of AIDS in Ireland.* Dublin: National Disease Surveillance Centre.

O'Dwyer, P. (2001). The Irish and substance abuse. In Straussner, S.L.A. (Ed.). *Ethnocultural Factors in the Treatment of Addictions* (pp. 199-215). New York: Guilford

O'Higgins, K. and Duff, P. (1997). *Treated Drug Misuse in Ireland: First National Report.* Dublin: The Health Research Board.

O'Higgins, K. (1998). *Review of literature and policy on the links between poverty and drug abuse.* Dublin: The Economic and Social Research Institute and the Combat Poverty Agency.

O'Mahony, P. (1997). *Mountjoy Prisoners: A sociological and criminological profile.* Dublin: Stationery Office.

Probation and Welfare Officers Branch, IMPACT (Public Sector) Union (1997), *The Management of the Drug Offender in Prison or on Probation.* Dublin: IMPACT Union.

Ritzer, G. (1993). *The McDonaldization of Society.* London: Thousand Oaks.

Shaw, S., Cartwright, A., Spratley, T. and Harwin, J. (1978). *Responding to Drinking Problems.* London: Croom Helm.

Skehill, C. (1999). *The Nature of Social Work in Ireland: A historical perspective.* Lewiston, NY: Edwin Mellen Press.

Stivers, R. (2000). *Hair of the Dog: Irish Drinking and Its American Stereotype* (New Revised Edition). New York: Continuum.

Woods, M. (2000). The Value of the Strengths Perspective in Understanding and Responding to Alcohol and Drugs Problems. *Irish Social Worker*, 18 (1), 20-22.

Dutch Drug Policy and the Role of Social Workers

Peter de Koning
Alex de Kwant

SUMMARY. Dutch drug policy has been renowned because of its pragmatic and liberal approach, and its positive effects on the health status and mortality rate of hard drug addicts. This policy, however, has had some negative consequences, especially with respect to crime and safety in big cities. As a result, the government took measures to redress these problems. This article presents an overview of recent measures in health care and criminal justice in the Netherlands and discusses the role of social work in drug addiction. *[Article copies available for a fee from The Haworth Document Delivery Service: 1-800-HAWORTH. E-mail address: <getinfo@haworthpressinc.com> Website: <http://www.HaworthPress.com> © 2002 by The Haworth Press, Inc. All rights reserved.]*

KEYWORDS. Drug policy in the Netherlands, health care, Dutch criminal justice, role of social work

INTRODUCTION

From its beginning in the early 1970s, the Dutch drug policy was characterised by pragmatism and leniency. This approach deviated

Peter de Koning and Alex de Kwant are both at the School of Socio-Legal Services at the Ichthus Professional University in Rotterdam, the Netherlands (E-mail: <p.dkoning@ichtus-hs.nl> and <l.dekwant@ichtus-hs.nl>).

[Haworth co-indexing entry note]: "Dutch Drug Policy and the Role of Social Workers." de Koning, Peter, and Alex de Kwant. Co-published simultaneously in *Journal of Social Work Practice in the Addictions* (The Haworth Social Work Practice Press, an imprint of The Haworth Press, Inc.) Vol. 2, No. 3/4, 2002, pp. 49-68; and: *International Aspects of Social Work Practice in the Addictions* (ed: Shulamith Lala Ashenberg Straussner, and Larry Harrison) The Haworth Social Work Practice Press, an imprint of The Haworth Press, Inc., 2002, pp. 49-68. Single or multiple copies of this article are available for a fee from The Haworth Document Delivery Service [1-800-HAWORTH, 9:00 a.m. - 5:00 p.m. (EST). E-mail address: getinfo@haworthpressinc.com].

49

from the one in most other countries–especially in its first two decades. This policy was the result of the specific circumstances of the period in which drug use (and misuse) became a problem, and of the specific structure and culture of political decision making in the Netherlands (Kort, 1996; Leuw, 1996). The emerging youth culture in the sixties, and various political and social movements demanded openness to new ideas from the traditional elites, and reflected the growing influence of various minorities in legislative and administrative settings. Although the police, and the judicial and governmental authorities did react with repressive measures, and the protest movement caused considerable political turmoil, generally speaking, the social criticism of these years was taken seriously.

This dual approach, of repression and openness to change, which characterized Dutch response at that time was also reflected with respect to the drug problem. At a time that prison sentences of a couple of months for the possession of even a few grams of marihuana were not uncommon, the government also installed two committees to study the problem and to advise the government about policy and legislative measures. This latter action was an example of the Dutch tradition in political decision-making. Serious problems tend to be de-politicised, rephrased in a neutral problem statement, and handed over to a committee of experts to inform the legislator about how to respond to the problem at hand. Although one committee came to more liberal conclusions than the other, both committee reports paved the way for a more or less unbiased approach to a relatively new problem–the appearance of drug dealers, users, and addicts in the streets.

This article concentrates on the changes in the criminal justice and treatment policy and the role of social work practice with respect to hard drug users and addicts. Other addictions and drug use, such as the use of alcohol and cannabis products, are addressed only briefly.

DUTCH DRUG POLICY IN THE 20TH CENTURY

The committee reports requested by the Dutch government to address the growing drug use were published in 1972 and their conclusions eventually resulted in a political compromise to revise the Dutch Opium Act in 1976. Since that time, the keywords in the legal and policy arenas with respect to drugs have been 'normalisation' and 'harm reduction.' The measures aimed at the separation of the markets of so-called "soft" (primarily cannabis products like marihuana and hashish) and "hard" drugs (such as cocaine and heroin). The use and small scale trade of the former was taken for granted. This policy approach implied, for instance, with the putting up with the existence of "coffee-shops" selling small amounts of cannabis-products for individual consumption, and of the existence of some free-zones or premises in which consumption of heroin and cocaine was tolerated. Smuggling and large scale traffic of both soft and hard drugs (the latter also with respect to the selling of small amounts) were, however, tracked down and prosecuted whenever possible.

With respect to abusers of hard drugs, the policy aimed at harm reduction. Addiction to hard drugs was seen as a social and medical problem, not as a criminal one. The Dutch harm-reduction policy was first and foremost targeted at protecting the physical health of the addicts themselves and reducing the possible risks of needle sharing, promiscuous behaviour, and prostitution, and preventing infectious diseases like hepatitis and HIV. The primary goal was to manage the drug problem and to contain it within the limits set by personal and public health.

Up to a point it can be argued that this policy was successful. The health-status and mortality rate of Dutch drug addicts is comparatively good (see Vogt, this volume) and the relatively easy access to cannabis products in the "coffee-shops" prevents new users (in general, adolescents) from contact with dealers of hard drugs like heroin and cocaine. In the Netherlands, drug addicts are not stigmatised as criminals just because of their addiction. However, despite these positive results, this policy did have some drawbacks, which became apparent in the middle of the 1980s (Second Chamber, 1994-1995; Swierstra, 1994). One was the attractiveness of the Dutch drug market to foreign users, and the relatively public, open nature of this market. The second, and the more important drawback, resulted from having the inhabitants of the poorer quarters in the big cities objected more and more to the adverse effects of this lenient policy approach since drug-dealings, petty crimes and other kinds of nuisance and 'indecent' behaviour of the addicts became common in these neighbourhoods. This elicited serious objections from the inhabitants, eventually leading to mild forms of citizen rebellion and taking the law into their own hands. Local legislators and policy-makers responded with more police surveillance and greater repression of drug traffic and use.

On top of the internal pressures from public opinion and municipal politicians, Dutch pragmatism and leniency became subject to severe international criticism, notably from USA, French and Swedish politicians and government agencies. This was further reinforced by the unification of the European market and the removal of national borders and custom controls, as well as a growing world-wide movement of anti-liberal moral values with respect to drugs. The First United Nations World Conference on Drugs (June, 1998) is a case in point: According to the presidents of the United States and France the 'war on drugs' has to be intensified. Furthermore, in the middle of the 1990s, a sharp political dispute between the French president and the Dutch government about drug policy seriously hindered Dutch efforts to establish a European drug policy based on the Dutch model, and put the Netherlands in a rather isolated political position (Leuw & Haen Marshall, 1996: x).

Another, probably unintended, consequence of the harm-reduction and market-separation policy was the neglect of the treatment of addiction and the rehabilitation of addicts. Reduction in the number of addicts was not an avowed policy goal, as this was seen as too ambitious (Leuw & Haen Marshall, 1996: xv). Besides, from the end of the 1980s the number of heroin addicts appeared to stabilise. Moreover, cessation of drug use was considered to be a matter of personal preference and motivation. To be sure, detoxification clinics, therapeutic communities, methadone maintenance, and treatment programmes have been part and parcel of the budgets for physical and mental health of the central and municipal governments. Addicts enter and leave these clinics and programmes, sometimes more than once, some with greater success than others. The large majority participates of its own volition, that is, without insistence, let alone compulsion, from legal authorities. Neither the use, nor the possession of small amounts of any kind of drug, is in itself a sufficient reason for arrest and prosecution. Being addicted to an illegal substance, then, is not enough of a cause for referral to treatment programmes by a public prosecutor or a judge.

As a result of the criticism of the existing policy in general, and the awareness of the gap in treatment possibilities in particular, the Dutch government proposed several additional measures. The measures were announced in a government memorandum addressed to parliament: *The Drug Policy of the Netherlands, Continuity and Change* (Second Chamber, 1994-1995). Contrary to the expectations of many, induced by the socialist-liberal character of the coalition, this memorandum did not propose to liberalise drug policy any further. Instead, the measures can be (and are) viewed as a retreat from the existing pragmatic course, and as giving in to the urge for more repression. The theme of all measures is the redressing of drug related crime and other drug related problems, ranging from organised large-scale drug trafficking to the vomiting of a homeless addict while on a public transport.

POLICIES REGARDING THE USES OF ALCOHOL AND SOFT DRUGS

From a historical point of view, most Dutch agencies that are now handling different kinds of addictions–to illicit drugs, gambling, medications, and more recently, to surfing the internet–started as detoxification and counselling agencies for alcohol addicts. When drug addiction became a problem in the late 1960s, the government as well as the agencies themselves, took for granted that the existing organisations were the ones to treat this new category of clients. Very quickly, the addiction to illicit drugs surpassed alcohol addiction in the attention of policy, treatment, and within the social work profession (Baal, Berg, & Swinkels, 1997; Vermeulen, 1997). In the middle of the 1990s approximately 200,000 persons were seriously addicted to alcohol, of which about ten percent were in treatment. The number of hard drug addicts amounted to roughly 30,000, of which 90 percent were in treatment (most of them, however, in the low profile intervention of methadone programmes). The yearly available budget per addicted client was about 220 euros for alcohol addicts, and 3,000 euros for drug addicts.

Another difference relates to government policy with respect to the regulation of the supply, demand, and possession of alcohol. From a legal point of view, there were no restrictions or regulations related to alcohol. Only during the last two years has the selling of alcohol to minors become prohibited, and a publicity campaign has been launched to reduce the alcohol consumption of young people. These measures, however, did not stem primarily from concern about alcohol addiction among youngsters, but with the increasing alcohol-related violence on the weekends. From a cynical point of view, one could say that the almost one billion euros of excise duties on alcoholic drinks far outweigh the efforts of the treatment agencies to detoxify the alcohol addicts.

Currently, with the first serious cases of addiction to cannabis products appearing in the Netherlands, the policies regarding the use and selling of soft drugs are also becoming less liberal. The "coffee-shops" are more strictly regulated than previously, and their number has been halved in the last five years. Those remaining have become subject to local rules concerning location (e.g., not in the neighbourhoods of schools), opening hours, construction and equipment, and police and administrative supervision.

THE CHANGING ROLE OF CRIMINAL JUSTICE AND DRUG TREATMENT

Before presenting a brief overview of the measures taken within the criminal justice system, and with respect to treatment programmes and the changing role of social work, we will present two cases, James and John, to illustrate the problems that have to be tackled. While the names of the persons in the examples are fictitious, their stories real and are derived from interviews with these individuals by one of the authors (Koning, 1998; Koning & Hessing, 2000).

The Case of James

James migrated from Surinam as an infant with his mother, stepfather, brothers and sisters to live in Rotterdam. Ten years later, the family returned to Surinam, but two years later decided to go back to the Netherlands when the political situation there became unstable following the military coup in 1982. They resettled in an old inner city neighbourhood, characterised by a multi-ethnic and low income population, poor housing conditions, and high rates of unemployment and crime. The family broke up, the mother and stepfather divorced, and the children did not get along with mother's new boyfriend. James did not resume school, ran away from home, and slept by turns at his mother's or stepfather's home, on the street, or with street friends. At the ages of fourteen and fifteen he was arrested several times for burglary and armed robbery. The juvenile court put him under the supervision of a tutor of the child welfare council, and ultimately placed him in community homes, all to no avail.

At that time James was not addicted to drugs, although he had been smoking marihuana daily ever since his early adolescence during the family's stay in Surinam. In 1985, in his mid-adolescence, he started dealing heroin and cocaine, and quickly moved up in the chain of drug trafficking. In the early years he himself did not use these drugs, and, probably because of that, managed to stay out of trouble with the police. This changed when he started using drugs and was no longer able to limit his use to the weekends. At the end of the 1980s, James was arrested when the police raided his dealing house, and from the withdrawal symptoms while in custody he could not deny any longer that he was addicted to heroin.

James served a couple of months in jail, and after his release decided to resume his life as a burglar and robber instead of dealing drugs. His expectation that in doing so he would make more money appeared to be true, but at the same time, his risk of arrests increased. From 1990 onwards he lived the life of a homeless, criminal drug addict, supporting himself with all kinds of property offences, which at times included violence. He became a regular visitor to police stations, courts and prisons, and was incarcerated ten to twelve times, ranging from a few weeks up to more than two years. His police file contains almost 100 major criminal offences, not counting minor ones. All in all, he has spent about ten years in prisons.

Most of the time he continued to use drugs while incarcerated. In 1994 and 1995 he requested transfer to a drug-free unit to participate in a prison-based treatment programme. After two failures, he succeeded in arranging after-care treatment upon release and managed to stay clean for more than one year. He relapsed again when his counsellor left the treatment service because of internal conflicts and reorganisation, and when he thought his new girlfriend became too interfering and demanding.

Within one year he was arrested again, sentenced to 13 months imprisonment, released, and within 20 days re-arrested for a minor offence. James was well aware of the downward spiral in the life he was living and the impossibility of a non-educated, homeless black man, who never had a regular job to break this vicious cycle. He requested the judge not to sentence him again to jail but to allow him to participate in a newly started compulsory treatment programme.

The Case of John

By the time of his last arrest John was a heavy user of licit and illicit substances. If he had enough money, he used one to three grams of heroin a day, up to five grams of cocaine (crack or raw), and 50 to 70 milligrams of methadone from the maintenance programme. He also used other substances, including tranquilisers, ecstasy and marihuana on a regular basis. He does not know why he started using drugs; maybe because of his problems with authority, his proclivity for excitement and aberrant behaviour, and the closeness of the drug scene. He did not experience serious family problems prior to his use. While his way of life caused many conflicts with his parents, they remained basically supportive.

Despite his heavy use of marihuana and alcohol, and (in the beginning) infrequent use of cocaine he finished an agricultural secondary school and earned good money working hard in regular and irregular jobs as a farmhand until his early twenties. At that time his drug use and criminal activities increased rapidly and remained problematic for the next 15 years. When not incarcerated or in a therapeutic community, he kept himself busy with burglary, fencing stolen goods, dealing cocaine, blackmail, and guarding the leaders of a drug traffic gang. His registered criminal record is substantial, his unregistered one even more so. His total time of incarceration amounted to ten years, varying from a half a year to three years.

John participated in several therapeutic communities, however all efforts to break with his addiction failed almost immediately. He refused to humiliate himself in front of the encounter group, and to recognise the community's hierarchy of authority. Besides, he could not resist the tempting excitement and money of the drug scene. Only once he succeeded in completing a programme and to remain more or less drug free for about two years. In this case, an enduring cohabitation with a girlfriend probably reinforced the therapy.

New Policies in Criminal Justice: Compulsory Diversion to Treatment

James and John are two typical representatives of hard-core criminal drug addicts whom the Dutch drug policy could not adequately handle until recently. Neither the penal system, nor the health care and treatment services provided effective methods and facilities to address the problems they posed to themselves, their families and the wider society. With few exceptions, each arrest and imprisonment and each interrupted or completed treatment programme was followed by new periods of addiction and crimes to support themselves and their habit. Apart from the abundant availability of drugs in prisons, the sentences were generally too short, and prison personnel did not have enough expertise and resources to provide treatment during custody. The well-intended efforts in drug-free units lacked any aftercare provisions. Upon release from prison, the addict had to rely mostly on himself to find work, housing, and to restore his family relation. Entry to therapeutic communities, detoxification clinics or other treatment programmes generally was voluntary, and the response of these communities and programmes towards those breaking internal rules, relapse and re-entry was rigid and stern. Consequently, few people with criminal histories used these services. Addicts used health care provisions, especially methadone maintenance, to cope with withdrawal symptoms and other adverse effects of addiction. In times of scarcity, of drugs or the money to buy it, methadone was abused as just another drug, one that was very cheap and easily accessible.

At the beginning of the 1990s various proposals were made in parliamentary papers to address the relationship between drugs and crime. At that time, the Dutch criminal and penal laws did not provide the option to compel drug addicts to long-term treatment. Even those sentenced to prison could not be coerced to engage in any kind of treatment. At most, participation was conditional upon a suspended sentence with parole or a probation term, but here too there was free choice: one could always opt for imprisonment. Since April 1, 2001 the criminal laws were changed to allow the judge to sentence an addict to compulsory placement in a prison-based treatment programme, irrespective the motivation or wishes of the addict.

The concept of "compulsory treatment programme" does not convey the specific meaning and character of the programme. Under Dutch law only persons who are mentally very disturbed and pose a serious danger for themselves or for society can be treated against their will. The majority of drug addicts do not qualify under these conditions. What can be compelled, then, is not the treatment itself, but the placement in a treatment programme. Because of this, the more adequate terms for this approach are "compulsory diversion" or "treatment under criminal justice supervision" (see Lipton, 1995).

Description of a Compulsory Diversion Programme

The programme presented here is based upon outcome research of a pilot criminal diversion project in Rotterdam (for more information, see Hoekstra, 1997; Koning, 1998; Municipality of Rotterdam, 1996). Not all addicts are eligible for this judicial intervention. It applies only to those persons who have been addicted for long term (more than five years), are arrested for an offence that permits for preventive custody, have been held in preventive custody previously during the year before the present arrest, and have been sentenced within the last two years. Furthermore, they have to be legal residents of the Netherlands. Addicts convicted of serious crimes, illegal foreign addicts, and those with serious psychiatric problems are excluded from this programme. In practise, these legal criteria restrict eligibility to poly-drug-abusing, and anti-social, often aggressive, men who have not responded to penal reactions and previous voluntary treatment. The few female addicts who are eligible for the programme will eventually be placed in a separate facility.

The goal of the programme is twofold. First, to reduce criminality related to drug abuse, and prevent further increase of addiction-related deviant behaviour by this relatively small, but notorious criminal category of addicts. The second goal is to rehabilitate the addicts causing these problems. The programme's emphasis is on physical labour, sports, social skills and more or less spontaneous group dynamics as ways to enhance self-discipline and self-esteem. During a period of complete and half-open confinement, new perspectives on housing and employment are offered, and, if necessary further education and treatment are provided. All this is expected to lead to a more normal, more civilised life after finishing the programme.

Those who qualify have to serve a long-term placement in the treatment facility (one and a half up to two years), instead of the typical shorter-term imprisonment, which usually does not exceed nine months. A deputy attorney and a probation officer inform the eligible addict about this option once he is arrested and held in remand at a police station. The probation officer makes a report to advice the judge about the individual's suitability and chances of success in the programme.

The placement consists of three stages. The first phase lasts six months and its primary goal is detoxification, recovering physical and mental health, and getting used to the routines and discipline of a normal daily, and later on, more laborious life. The participants are trained to show adequate social behaviour and to take responsibility for personal conduct. Programme activities include various kind of work in and around the premises, sports, and elementary or, if possible, vocational schooling. Most of the activities are carried out in a group of at the most ten participants with whom the addict is placed when entering the programme. During the first phase, the participant is kept in total confinement.

In the second phase, which lasts from six to nine months, the focus is on vocational training and obtaining job experience. Running the household for and with the group is also an important task and a skill to be acquired. Two other important elements during this phase are learning useful and pleasant leisure activities without the use of drugs or excessive drinking, and restoring relations with family and, if possible, with friends outside the drug scene. After six weeks, the participant may gradually be allowed time off in the evenings and weekends to spend outside the residential premises.

During the third phase, which also lasts a period of six to nine months, participants must leave the premises of the programme and are placed in normal houses or rooms, and, if they have not been able to find a job by themselves, in work projects sponsored by the programme. During this phase the actual return to the normal society and a more civilised life is accomplished, although the individual is still under strict control and guidance of the probation officer.

Research on the compulsory treatment programme will not yield substantial outcomes before the end of 2003. A study of the first one and a half years of the experimental pilot programme found that by the end of March 1998, 102 persons have been placed in the programme, with 46 percent still participating (Koning, 1998). Forty percent of the drop-outs left within a month, sixty percent within three months. Most were incarcerated after leaving the programme. The relapse among program drop-outs is substantial: 32 of the 55 drop-outs were found to have new felonies (three, on average), all of the 32 and ten of the other drop-outs are known to have resumed drug use. Five years after the start of the experimental programme, about 15 percent of all participants that completed the programme are drug free and crime free six months after release. This figure is not substantially higher than that found in voluntary treatment programmes (personal communication of the director of the experimental programme to one of the authors, April 2001).

Follow-up research will reveal whether the remaining participants will abstain from criminal activities and be able to control their drug use. In the meantime, programme participation implies the prevention of a large number of property offences, since the participants are not out on the streets. The average number of crimes per person per year, in combination with estimates of the material damage resulting from those offences and discounting for the drop-outs, gives some idea of the financial benefits of the treatment programme. Therefore, despite the low success rate, it appears that treatment under criminal justice supervision is almost 40 percent more cost effective than the policy of arrest, prosecution, sentencing, incarceration and methadone maintenance (Koning, 1998; Koning & Hessing, 2000).

CHANGING HEALTH CARE INITIATIVES

Medical Prescription of Heroin

Despite the generally positive health and mortality rates resulting from the current Dutch drug policy, a small marginalised group of addicts roam the streets, too decompensated to even live the life of a criminal. These individuals have been addicted for a very long time, are homeless, relatively old, and chronically ill. Since rehabilitation based on eliminating their drug addiction is not a realistic option for them, they are eligible for heroin prescription. The aim is to enable them to lead an almost normal life without the need to raise illegal money to support their habit. In this way their criminal, economical and social costs are greatly reduced.

The dispensing of heroin was started in 1998 as an experimental study to examine whether the medical prescription of heroin is a feasible, desirable and functional alternative to the existing medical interventions with drug addicts (Health Council of the Netherlands 1995; Garretsen et al. 1996; Joint Municipal Health Agencies 1996). It was primarily designed as a palliative measure for the individual addict, in order to reduce the health risks and to regulate and to stabilise his or her way of living. Furthermore, this experiment is designed to provide insight into the effects of the prescription on the nature and course of the addiction, and the supplementary use of heroin and other drugs. It is obvious that this approach is not intended to detoxify the addict. However, if the medical experiment succeeds, and palliation and stabilisation are reached, additional rehabilitative and treatment programmes will be offered in order to induce the addicts to abstain completely, and to turn their anti-social behaviour into a more responsible life style. This is one of the few times in which science-based evidence is sought about the outcomes of implementing medical prescription. Because of the political sensitivity of this project, however, no interim findings will be published; the first results of this experiment are not expected before the end of 2002.

For this study, medical officers of the municipal health agencies of six cities, including Amsterdam and Rotterdam, selected 750 hard drug addicts from the target population. To be eligible, the addict needed to have had a long-term addiction to heroin; have previously failed in methadone maintenance and other treatment programmes; suffer from poor physical health; have serious problems with psychological and social functioning; be at least 25 years of age; and be officially registered as an inhabitant of the municipalities implementing the experiment.

From the total sample of 750, three sub-samples, one experimental and two control groups, were randomly selected. The prescribed heroin is being administered to the experimental group during a period of one year. One control group is receiving the standard methadone treatment for half a year, after which it also will become an experimental group for one year. The other control group will remain in the methadone programme during the whole experimental programme. Afterwards they will be considered for prescription of heroin as a kind of reward for their co-operation and in order to prevent them from dropping out during the experiment. All groups are being compared with respect to their physical and mental health, psychological well-being, participation in society, and additional drug use.

Other Treatment Initiatives

This section will describe some of the initiatives and projects that have been undertaken by agencies for addiction, mental health institutes and patient/client groups during the second half of the 1990s. Some of the initiatives received a lot of attention in the media, and were highly debated in public, especially the establishment of user-friendly places, and the temporary employment agency for drug users, Top Score. Others have a relatively low profile, like the local care networks, case management and assertive outreach programmes.

Whereas the policies discussed previously come top-down from the national government, and in the end should have a nation-wide more or less uniform implementation, the initiatives discussed here have a more bottom-up character, and are implemented in cooperation with the local governments. This implies that the existence, the number, and the kinds of initiatives vary among municipalities and agencies and are coloured by the peculiarities of the local situation, by their perception of the addiction problem and by their ways of approaching it. All aim, however, at integrating the care for the addicts and restoring and maintaining public order. Which goal is on the forefront of a particular project depends on the nature of the agencies involved in the project (Wolf, 2001). If it is the local government, the emphasis is on the reduction of public annoyance and restoring trust in public safety. If the initiatives are established by addiction treatment facilities or those concerned with mental health, the emphasis is on harm reduction. Those projects initiated by patient/client groups, like the Junkie Union, emphasise the normalisation of drug use and addiction.

User-Friendly Places. Despite the emphasis on the reduction of public annoyance in national and local politics, there has been an increase in what has been termed "user-friendly" places in the early 1990s. These places were designed to offer long-term addicted street users a place to take their drugs in a relatively safe environment. Their main goals are harm reduction and the reduction of drug related annoyance in public places.

Although their number has increased recently, user-friendly places are not new; the 19th century opium dens are an early example of the same phenomenon. The difference is that the setting up of the present places is encouraged, and sometimes organised, by detoxification and municipal health agencies. Often an agreement is reached with the local government, police authorities and neighbourhood representatives to tolerate such user-friendly places as long as the dealers and the users do not cause trouble.

Three types of user-friendly places can be distinguished: informal, integrated and specific (Graaf et al., 2001). The *informal place* is run by dealers or former drug users and can be found in every part of the Netherlands, mainly in the larger cities. Its sole purpose is to provide a relatively quite environment where the user can buy and inject or smoke the heroin or cocaine. These places are not connected with drug treatment agencies, and are tolerated by the police and city administration as long as the dealers and users refrain from criminal or annoying behaviour. If they do cause problems, the facility is closed temporarily or even permanently.

Most of the user-friendly places in the Netherlands fall into the category of *integrated places*. These places combine an already existing shelter for the homeless or for drug addicts with a facility with more extended services. *Specific places* are those visited mostly by a subgroup of users, who want to have nothing to do with the regular institutes or agencies for addiction. They are frequently visited by the so-called "care avoiding problematic drug addicts." These addicts suffer physical, mental, psychiatric and legal problems, and deliberately shun the health care and treatment programmes, with the exception of methadone programs. Using assertive outreach, places such as St. Paul's Church in Rotterdam, provide various services, such as day care, medical care, and shelter. Their aim is not the normalisation of drug use, but on the normalisation of the drug user.

Local-Care Networks. In 1992 several social work and mental health agencies became concerned about the growing number of people with complex problems, such as the drug using, mentally ill homeless individuals who were squatting in empty houses and causing various kinds of public annoyance (Poodt & Wierdsma, 1999). This concern resulted in the establishment of "local-care networks," a collaboration between the municipal administration, welfare and mental health agencies and the centre for addictions. Currently, in Rotterdam there are seven local-care networks, distributed all over the city; comparable initiatives can be found in other cities in the Netherlands. Basically, all these initiatives are similar, but the Rotterdam approach aims at a wider group of people, such as the hard to reach drug users. The approach involved the use of assertive outreach, a method developed for long-term psychiatric patients. This method emphasises case management and care broker-age, and presupposes that it is the worker, and not the client/patient who is responsible for initiating the care and treatment relationship.

Housing for the Elderly Drug User. As a result of the Dutch drug pol-icy and treatment, the drug user population reaching pension age is growing. In 1999, the city of Rotterdam made headlines with the open-ing of a housing facility for elderly drug users. This was an initiative of the *Junkie Union,* a consumer run organisation, aiming at furthering the interests of the drug user and the normalisation of the drug use. This ini-tiative was also supported by the Municipal Health Agency and the main detoxification and drug treatment centres.

The need for such specialised shelter was born out of two assump-tions: the first was that the regular institutions for elderly would reject the elderly drug users, fearing opposition by the families of other elders in their care. The second assumption was that elderly drug users should have a place where they were allowed to use drugs, while being pro-tected against the hardships of the drug scene on the streets. This initia-tive can also be considered as a kind of local care network, with the *Junkie Union* providing for a house dealer who visits the occupants on a daily basis, and with the health agency and a drug treatment centre pro-viding medical and social care. About ten drug users are currently housed in this old age facility.

Top Score. Three years earlier it was also the Rotterdam *Junkie Union* that started an agency for temporary employment of drug us-ers, *Top Score.* The name of this project is a wordplay, as *scoring* is one of the basic activities in the world of the drug user. The Top Score project offers drug users the possibility of supplementing their benefits with earned income in order to prevent them from falling back into crime, and offering them the potential for a new purpose in life. At the start, more than one hundred drug users applied for jobs. After a few months the project succeeded in employing a few dozens of users in municipal and public transport cleansing departments, where they clean streets, parks, subway stations and other public places in Rotterdam. Currently, small groups of drug users sweeping the streets and squares dressed in yellow or orange overalls are com-monly seen in the city.

THE CHANGING ROLE FOR SOCIAL WORK

The relationship between policymakers and the social work profession in the drug field has been troublesome from the moment the Dutch government developed a drug policy. To be sure, in the various private and public agencies implementing this policy–from user-friendly places to prisons–hundreds of social workers are employed as clinical workers in residential treatment, in out-patient clinics, or as street corner workers. In fact they are the largest category of employees in addiction treatment (Baal et al., 1997; Kersten, 1998). But they were seldom at the leading edge in the making or implementing of drug policies, either at the micro level of individual practice or at the macro level of the profession as a whole.

One reason for this limited role of social work is that the national government has never issued a policy statement that addressed the social work role in the drug field. From its inception, drug policy was seen in medical terms, emphasising harm reduction and the prevention of damage to public health and to the physical and mental health status of the drug users. As a consequence, it has been primarily the medical doctors, epidemiologists, psychiatrists and nursing professionals who defined and provided the services needed by the drug users, such as needle exchange, methadone treatment, health check-ups, and therapeutic interventions.

The separation of the so-called hard drugs (heroin, cocaine) from the soft drugs (cannabis) was also considered from the harm reduction perspective, which did not include social work interventions but was focused on efforts to control the supply, the demand and the use of the different kinds of drugs. The other cornerstone of the Dutch drug policy, normalisation, also did not invite social workers to play an active role. With some exaggeration, one could state that the normalisation policy was a large publicity campaign aiming at accepting drug use as a normal phenomenon in society. By doing so, however, it weakened the moral argument that would sanction any role of social work in trying to interfere with the habits of the drug users.

These policy objectives resulted in comparatively little attention to the rehabilitation of addicts. Treatment programmes were targeted primarily at detoxification, which was also defined as a medical problem. Health care interventions and social work interventions were arrayed in a time order, with social work services always provided after the primary focus on health. Since treatment was voluntary, drug users frequently left the treatment facility after detoxification without entering a rehabilitation programme run by the social work department in the facility. Consequently, addiction related problems such as poverty, unemployment, homelessness, problems with the police, and disturbed relationships with family and friends, were not addressed. Neither were the repressed social and psychological problems causing the addiction, which got covered up for years under a blanket of narcotics.

A third reason for the relatively limited role of social work has to do with the professional status of the social work profession itself (Kersten, 1998), which until very recently had not achieved an academic status in the Netherlands. The highest educational degree offered in social work is the BA degree, and the educational programme is highly influenced by a generalist professional practice. There are hardly any specialties or majors in the addiction field at the BA level of education of social workers. The absence of an academic tradition contributed to the lack of evaluation studies of social work interventions, which in turn precluded educational programmes from any systematic learning about social work practice. Treatment and care interventions have all been based on trial and error since research-based standards and guidelines for treatment matching, referral and therapeutic interventions are lacking. While social workers work in all kind of treatment agencies and programmes, they do not share a broadly accepted professional philosophy regarding their role in the addiction field. It is the programmes or agencies in which they work that define their view on addiction and the way to approach it.

Things, however, appear to be changing. These changes have not so much to do with the kind of agency, or treatment programme social workers are involved in, but more with their role in, and contribution to, these agencies and programmes. Whereas the normalisation and harm reduction policy implied a passive, wait and see role of social workers, the recent emphasis on disciplining and rehabilitation, as part and parcel of the urban safety policy, requires a more active role involving outreach to this population. Furthermore, within the next few years, social work interventions will be based much more thoroughly on research findings. The department of Health and Welfare and the Department of Justice are promoting and funding social work research programmes to evaluate the various medical, social work and criminal justice interventions, and to develop standards, guidelines and protocols for matching clients and programmes (Kersten, 1998).

Social work role is currently more prominent than before in all the programs discussed previously, with the exception of the heroin prescription programme. But even there, a supplementary rehabilitation programme run by social workers and focusing on improvement of social skills and restoring social relations is offered. In the compulsory treatment programme this is taken a few steps further, as social group workers try to change the behaviours of the addicts and trigger their motivation to live a life without drugs. Probation officers act as case managers, organising all kinds of interventions including medical care, elementary education, vocational training, housekeeping, sports and other recreational activities. Also, the number of social workers, as well as the quality of their contribution is expected to increase as more local-care networks and user-friendly facilities are established.

One final factor will further influence the role and position of social work in the addiction field, and that is the fact that programmes and initiatives are not developed in isolation. Most are part and parcel of the national urban safety and renewal policy, aiming at rehabilitating deteriorated neighbourhoods, redressing the poverty of their inhabitants, and coping with problems of a multi-ethnic society. While the Dutch government was cutting the budgets for social work during the last quarter of the 20th century, the need for social work interventions increased. The influx of large groups of immigrants, the moving of middle and upper class inhabitants to suburban areas, and the changing nature of the economic basis of big cities, all led to rising unemployment, greater impoverishment and higher crime rates, as well as a decrease in the social cohesion in urban communities. Under such circumstances, a drug policy focusing exclusively on harm reduction and normalisation of drug use and addiction will no longer be effective. Other programmes aimed at improving communities and those more directed at increasing motivation to change will be needed. Social work professionals have the responsibility to develop, administer and to evaluate these programmes.

CONCLUSION

Dutch drug policy has been described as vacillating between repression and punishment on the one hand, and tolerance and treatment on the other. Currently, the policy is trying to find a third road "between prohibition and legalisation" (Leuw & Haen Marshall, 1996). Given the distinction between decriminalisation and legalisation, one could say that the Dutch drug policy has decriminalised soft drugs (Grapendaal et al., 1996; MacCoun, 1993; Second Chamber, 1994-1995). The recent medical prescription of heroin can be considered as a further step on this end of the continuum. Also, some of the social work initiatives, especially the establishment of user-friendly places and housing facility for elderly addicts, support this approach. At the same time, the new policy initiatives do not have to be based on repression of drug use in general, but on the improvement of the living condition in drug-prone inner city districts, and on increasing the rehabilitation chances of the addicts. Conditional upon the quality of the programme and the possibilities for long term after-care (Rigter, 1999), many addicts in the criminal justice can be placed in treatment against their will for a couple of months, which would allow them to detoxify and to consider the future course of their lives. In the end, it is the inherent motivation of the addict that will contribute to the success of a treatment programme. And, it is here that social workers can make a significant contribution.

REFERENCES

Baal, M. van, Berg, E. van den, Swinkels, H. (1997), Drank een groter probleem dan drugs. [Alcohol, a bigger problem than drugs.] *Index*, *4*(6).

Boekhout van Solinge, T. (1997), *The Swedish drug control system. An in-depth review and analysis*. Amsterdam: Jan Mets/Cedro

Graaf I. de, L. Linssen and J. Wolf (2001), Gebruiksruimten in Nederland. (User friendly places in the Netherlands) *Passage 10*(2).

Grapendaal, M., Leuw E. and Nelen, J.M. (1996), Legalization, decriminalization and the reduction of crime, In: E. Leuw and I. Haen Marshall (Eds.), *Between prohibition and legalization: The Dutch experiment in drug policy*, 233-253, Amsterdam/New York: Kugler.

Health Council of the Netherlands [Gezondheidsraad] (1995), *Het voorschrijven van heroïne aan verslaafden aan heroïne*. [The prescription of heroin to heroin addicts]. The Hague: Health Council of the Netherlands; publication no. 1995/12.

Hoekstra, A. (1997), Het experiment de strafrechtelijke opvang verslaafden. [The experiment with compulsory placement of addicts]. *Proces 76*(2).

Joint Municipal Health Agencies of Amsterdam, Rotterdam, The Hague, Utrecht a.o., [GG&GD Amsterdam, GGD Den Haag, GGD Rotterdam, GG&GD Utrecht and GGD Regio Stedendriehoek] (1996), *Basisdocument voor een onderzoek naar de effecten van gecontroleerde verstrekking van heroïne in Nederland* [Document for a study on the effects of controlled prescription of heroin in the Netherlands]. Amsterdam.

Kersten, G.C.M. (1998), Indicatiestelling en verwijzing in de verslavingszorg: Van intuïtie naar model. [Matching and referrals in addiction treatment: From intuition to modelling]. Ph.D. Thesis, Catholic University Nijmegen.

Koning, P. de (1998), *Resocialiseren onder drang. Verslag van het Rotterdams experiment met de strafrechtelijke opvang van verslaafden*. [Forced rehabilitation. Report on the Rotterdam experiment with treatment of hard drug addicts under penal law].

published by Erasmus Universiteit Rotterdam, Gemeente Rotterdam, and Stichting Opvang Verslaafden.

Koning P.J. de and D.J. Hessing (2000). Three ways to fight the drug problem: New approaches in the Dutch drug policy. In Nagel S.S. (Ed.), *Handbook of global legal policy.* 287-311, New York, Marcel Dekker Inc.

Kort, M. de (1996), A short history of drugs in the Netherlands. p. 3-22 in: Leuw, Ed. and I. Hean Marshall (Eds.), *Between prohibition and legalization. The Dutch experiment in drug policy.* Amsterdam / New York, Kugler Publications (2nd edition).

Leuw, E. (1996), Initial construction and development of the official Dutch drug policy. P. 23-40 in: Leuw, Ed. and I. Hean Marshall (Eds.), *Between prohibition and legalization. The Dutch experiment in drug policy.* Amsterdam / New York: Kugler Publications (2nd edition).

Leuw, E. and I. Haen Marshall (Eds.) (1996), *Between prohibition and legalization: The Dutch experiment in drug policy,* Amsterdam/New York: Kugler.

Lipton, D.S. (1995), The effectiveness of treatment for drug abusers under criminal justice supervision. Research Report of the U.S. National Institute of Justice. *Internet: <www.ncjrs.org/txtfiles/drugsupr.txt>.*

MacCoun, R.J. (1993), Drugs and the law: A psychological analysis of drug prohibition, *Psychological Bulletin,* Vol. 113, 497-512.

Municipality of Rotterdam [Bestuursdienst Rotterdam] (1996), *Van insluiting naar aansluiting. Een plan van aanpak t.b.v. het experiment strafrechtelijke opvang verslaafden* [From incarceration to connection. A plan of approach with regard to the experiment of penal treatment of addicts], Rotterdam.

Poodt H.D. & Wierdsma, I. (1999), *Lokale zorgnetwerken als panacee voor grootstedelijke problematiek.* [Local care networks as panacea for urban problems.] Municipal Health Agency of Rotterdam.

Rigter, H. (1999), Justitiële drang en dwang bij de behandeling van verslaafden: helpt het? [Judicial force and coercion in the treatment of addicts: does it work?]. p.24-28 in *Overlast. Een zorg voor Justitie en Zorg.* [Annoyance. A problem for criminal justice and social care agencies] Den Haag: Ministerie van Volksgezondheid, Welzijn en Sport.

Second Chamber of Parliament [Tweede Kamer der Staten-Generaal], (1994-1995), *Het Nederlandse drugbeleid: Continuïteit en verandering.* [Drug policy in the Netherlands: Continuity and change.] 24077, no. 2-3.

Swierstra, K.E. (1994), Drugsscenario's. Paars regeerakkoord, roze toekomstbeelden. [Drug scenario's. The programme of the new government, a rose-coloured picture of the future] *Justitiële Verkenningen, 20*(8): 115-143.

Vermeulen, E. (1997), Verslavingszorg en sociaal beleid. [Treatment of addictions and social policy] In: Schuyt, K. (Ed.) Het sociaal tekort [Shortcomings of the welfare state. 93-111, Amsterdam: De Balie].

Wolf, J., Begrip en beheersing van drugsoverlast [Understanding and controlling drug annoyance.] *Passage, 10*(2): 67-76.

Substance Use and Abuse and the Role of Social Workers in Germany

Irmgard Vogt

SUMMARY. The paper outlines major trends in consumption patterns of alcohol and other drugs in Germany with special focus on the use of cannabis among young people. It discusses primary prevention efforts and describes the current treatment system with its two branches: one for people with alcohol problems and the other for those with drug problems. It highlights the developing role of social work and identifies the research topics that are influenced by social workers and that will influence the debate regarding the future role of the profession. *[Article copies available for a fee from The Haworth Document Delivery Service: 1-800-HAWORTH. E-mail address: <getinfo@haworthpressinc.com> Website: <http://www.HaworthPress.com> © 2002 by The Haworth Press, Inc. All rights reserved.]*

KEYWORDS. Psychoactive drugs in Germany, alcohol and drug abuse, prevention and treatment systems, social work, research

INTRODUCTION

Germany with its population of 82 million people is the largest market place in Europe for psychoactive substances such as alcoholic bev-

Irmgard Vogt, PhD, Dipl Psych, is Professor at the University of Applied Sciences, Fachhochschule Frankfurt am Main, Fachbereich Soziale Arbeit und Gesundheit, Institut fuer Suchtforschung, Frankfurt am Main, Germany (E-mail: i.vogt@ soz.uni-frankfurt.de).

[Haworth co-indexing entry note]: "Substance Use and Abuse and the Role of Social Workers in Germany." Vogt, Irmgard. Co-published simultaneously in *Journal of Social Work Practice in the Addictions* (The Haworth Social Work Practice Press, an imprint of The Haworth Press, Inc.) Vol. 2, No. 3/4, 2002, pp. 69-83; and: *International Aspects of Social Work Practice in the Addictions* (ed: Shulamith Lala Ashenberg Straussner, and Larry Harrison) The Haworth Social Work Practice Press, an imprint of The Haworth Press, Inc., 2002, pp. 69-83. Single or multiple copies of this article are available for a fee from The Haworth Document Delivery Service [1-800-HAWORTH, 9:00 a.m. - 5:00 p.m. (EST). E-mail address: getinfo@haworthpressinc.com].

erages, cigarettes, prescribed medications and illicit drugs. Germans have long been notorious for their drinking habits and for their permissiveness toward drunken comportment, resulting in ever increasing numbers of alcohol addicts. Since the 1970s, there are also black markets for illicit drugs such as heroin and cocaine, and in its aftermath, a growing numbers of drug dependents. Social workers are deeply involved in providing professional help for substance dependents as will be described in detail below.

EPIDEMIOLOGICAL DATA ON THE USE AND ABUSE OF PSYCHOACTIVE SUBSTANCES

Data regarding the percentage of consumers of alcohol and of smokers of tobacco and cannabis show the importance of psychoactive substances in everyday life in Germany. The consumption patterns of different substances are of interest not only to market analysts and politicians, but also to public health professionals including social workers. As can be seen in Table 1, alcoholic beverages, tobacco and cannabis are widely used by people of all ages, particularly by the young. Young people typically begin to use psychoactive substances between the ages of 13 and 15. They usually start with alcoholic beverages at home and with cigarette smoking in peer groups. Later on, they move to experimenting with cannabis with their peers (Kleiber & Soellner 1998: Soellner 2000).

The Use of Cannabis

As in other European countries, cannabis is an illicit drug in Germany. Nevertheless, the percentage of men and women under the age of 30 who smoke cannabis, either on regular or irregular basis, is quite large, probably much larger than indicated by the data given in Table 1. Among university students, the percentage of life-time smokers of cannabis ranges between 50% and 75%, and the percentage of those who smoked it in the last 30 days is between 20% and 50% (Frieg & Lipp, 2001). In this population, the percentage of people who are smoking cannabis does not differ much from those smoking tobacco, leading to increasing pressure to decriminalize possession of small quantities of cannabis (up to 30 grams) and its occasional use.

Alcohol vs. Drug Dependence

Estimates of the number of people in Germany dependent on alcohol compared to those dependent on illicit drugs such as heroin, cocaine and related substances are provided in Table 2. It is estimated that 3% the population are alcohol dependent and 0.2% are drug dependent.

TABLE 1. Alcohol Consumers, Smokers of Tobacco and Cannabis by Age and Sex (in percent)

AGE	< 20		21-24		25-29		30-39		40-49		50-59	
SEX	M	F	M	F	M	F	M	F	M	F	M	F
Alcohol:[1] Abstainers	11.6	12.6	11.2	13.1	7.7	11.0	7.0	8.5	8.6	11.3	6.4	13.1
Very moderate Alc. Consumers	58.2	77.0	45.1	60.1	47.7	74.1	40.3	73.9	33.9	64.7	29.9	64.5
Moderate Alc. Consumers	20.0	9.0	30.0	20.5	30.6	10.6	41.1	11.7	43.1	15.1	41.9	14.6
Heavy Alc. Consumers	10.3	1.4	13.7	6.3	14.0	4.3	11.6	5.9	14.3	8.9	21.8	7.8
Smokers[2] Tobacco	22	14	44	32	47	35	48	41	40	31	33	19
Smokers[3] Cannabis	24.5	16.5	31.8	23.0	21.8	19.7	21.6	13.0	11.9	6.6	3.9	2.6

[1] Abstainers = no alcohol consumed in the last 12 months;
very moderate consumers = up to 10 Gr. of pure alcohol/per day (both sexes);
moderate consumers = men: up to 40 Gr. of pure alcohol/per day, women: up to 20 Gr. of pure alcohol/per day;
heavy consumers = men: > 40 Gr. of pure alcohol/per day, women: > 20 Gr. of pure alcohol/per day.
[2] Smokers of tobacco = persons who have smoked in the last 30 days.
[3] Smokers of cannabis = rates of life-time consumption.

TABLE 2. Estimates of Individuals Dependent on Alcohol and Illicit (hard) Drugs

	Men		Women		Total	
	N	%*	N	%*	N	%*
Alcohol	1,750,000	2.13	750,000	0.91	2,500,000	3.04
Illicit drugs	100,000	0.12	50,000	0.06	150,000	0.18

*Total population
Source: DHS (ed.): Jahrbuch Sucht, 1998

It is instructive to put the rate of drug dependence in Germany within the context of other European countries. As can be seen in Table 3, these rates are highest in Switzerland and lowest in the Netherlands. In northern countries including Switzerland, drug dependent men outnumber women by approximately 3:1, while in southern countries such as France and Spain, this ratio approaches 5 to1. Such sex ratio differences between northern and southern countries seems to reflect the more traditional gender role patterns in southern regions of Europe. It is not quite clear why these estimates of drug addicts vary so much among the different countries, even between neighboring countries such as Germany and Switzerland. Since these are not simply due to sampling differences, additional research is clearly needed.

Gender Differences

Boys and girls typically start drinking between the ages of 10 to 15. Normally, the very first drink is offered to them at home by their parents or relatives or during festivities. Between the ages of 16 and 20, gender differences in the preferred types of alcoholic beverages and in the quantity and frequency of consumption of alcohol become evident. Overall, young men prefer to drink beer on a daily basis, while young women prefer to drink wine on a weekly basis. The percentage of moderate and heavy drinking men increases considerably with age, and many begin to drink hard liquor in addition to beer. In the age range be-

TABLE 3. Estimates of Drug Dependent Men and Women in Selected European Countries

Country	Drug Dependents (per 100,000 inhabitants)		
	Total	Female	Male
Switzerland	461	115	346
Spain	258	43	215
Sweden	205	51	154
Germany*	205	59	146
France	181	30	151
Netherlands	164	47	117

*Former West Germany only
Source: Vogt, 1998

tween 30 and 60 years, alcohol abusing men outnumber women approximately by 3:1.

When it comes to smoking tobacco, gender differences are not very marked, particularly for those under the age of 50. Nonetheless, the overall percentage of men who smoke is somewhat higher than that of women, and males tend to be heavier smokers than women. Gender differences among smokers of cannabis, however, are quite large: significantly more men than women smoked it at least once in their lives, and significantly more men have been using it in the last 30 days (Kraus & Augustin, 2001; Kraus & Bauernfeind, 1998; Maschewski-Schneider, 1997).

In Germany, as in other European countries, alcohol dependence and more recently, drug dependence is more common among men (Vogt & Schmid, 1998). Thus, the very first treatment institutions for alcoholics, which were established between 1880 and 1900 (Martius, 1908), were for men only. At that time, except for stigmatizing remarks, women were not mentioned as having substance abuse problems. It took more or less another century for women to increase their consumption of alcoholic beverages and later-on of tranquilizers and sleeping pills. In the second half of the 20th century, alcohol abuse problems among women became evident as did their need for treatment. Soon, women abusing psychoactive medicines began asking for help, and finally those dependent on illicit drugs. Since the 1970s, the treatment system has been opened to both genders. However, due to its history, a gender bias is built into the treatment system, fitting it better to the needs of men than of women (Vogt, 1994, 2000).

PREVENTION AND TREATMENT APPROACHES

Primary Prevention and the Role of Social Workers

The idea of alcohol prevention programs and the diffusion of prevention messages is rather old, and first efforts date back to 1900. In the 1970s, a new prevention approach was developed focusing on the distribution of information regarding the dangerous effects of all psychoactive substances. Over the years, the prevention model changed from using scare techniques to utilizing empowerment concepts as promoted by the World Health Organization (WHO, 1986). This approach initially emphasized conflict management training, but quickly expanded to provide life skills training with little reference to psychoactive substances. Currently, the emphasis of primary prevention is shifting to include a mixture of information distribution techniques, identifying both the positive and negative effects of psychoactive substances, and life skills training (Röhrle & Sommer, 1999; Schmidt & Hurrelmann, 2000).

The main arenas used to promote preventive messages are schools and the mass media. The role of social workers in both of these areas is minimal. The most important actors in the schools are teachers, while in the mass media, it is public health professionals. Nonetheless, social work has its own niche in prevention. Social workers form special teams that are then invited into schools as experts and, together with teachers, prepare special workshops for schoolchildren. They build networks with local authorities to diffuse primary prevention messages outside schools and provide informative materials regarding the effects of illicit drugs at discos, raves and other events that attract large numbers of young people. In a few cities, they offer simple drug testing tools for those who want to check their drugs before consuming them. They also engage in secondary prevention via community youth work (Holinghorst, 2000). Overall, social work is a player in primary prevention, but not a very strong actor.

THE PROVISION OF TREATMENT, REHABILITATION AND AFTER CARE

The German treatment system for those who are dependent on substances has two branches: a large branch for those dependent on alcohol alone or in combination with psychoactive medicines such as tranquilizers, sleeping pills, etc., and a much smaller, but better differentiated, branch for those dependent on heroin and other illicit drugs, such as cocaine and crack. Unlike cocaine, crack is not very common in Germany. There is, however, one exception: in Frankfurt am Main it is crack, but not cocaine, that is used regularly by hard core addicts (Vogt & Schmid, 2000).

While those dependent on both alcohol and illicit drugs may use either of the branches of the treatment system, in reality they do so only if they have no other choice. For instance, outpatient facilities in the countryside offer counseling for both alcoholics as well as for drug addicts. However, the latter prefer to go to special facilities for drug addicts in the cities, which are better equipped for their needs. Individuals who are dependent on alcohol are usually less choosy and tend to take advantage

TABLE 4. German Outpatient and Inpatient Treatment System in 2000

Type of Institution	Number of Institutions	Number of Persons/Year	Number of Places/Beds
Outpatient facilities mainly for men and women with substance abuse problems	1,000-1,390	Ca. 300,000	
• Of those: specialized facilities for drug dependent men and women	150-400	N/A	ca. 500[1]
Of those: facilities for women with drug problems	ca. 20	N/A	ca. 50[1]
• Methadone dispensaries[2]	ca. 170	ca. 30,000	-
Detoxification centers (clinical wards) for men/	N/A	N/A	6,000-8,000
• Of those: detox centers for drug dependent men/women	N/A	N/A	ca. 1,500
Inpatient treatment centers, mainly for men and women with substance abuse problems[3]	N/A	ca. 70,000	ca. 15,000
• Of those: centers for drug dependent men/women	N/A	N/A	ca. 5,000
• Of those: centers for women with drug problems	ca. 10	N/A	ca. 100

[1] Refers to beds in day-and-night shelters.
[2] Refers to institutions in metropolitan areas only.
[3] Some inpatient treatment centers are for alcohol dependent men only, and a few are for women only. The majority of the centers take in men as well as women.
Sources: DHS (ed.): Jahrbuch Sucht, 2001, Vogt et al., 1998

of all the services offered to them. Conflicts between alcoholics and drug addicts are common in treatment centers in which both groups are together because of status differences between them. Drug addicts feel superior to alcohol addicts and tend to dominate the facilities as well as treatment groups. On the whole, drug addicts, in contrast to the alcoholics, are more aggressive when it comes to defending their own interests and meeting their needs.

Currently there are discussions regarding the merger of the two branches in order to reduce costs. Merging makes a lot of sense when it comes to outpatient facilities in smaller cities and rural areas, but not as much in metropolitan areas with their open drug scenes and the serious problems that go with them (cf. Krausz & Raschke, 1999). The discussion of merging the two branches is still in its beginning and may go on for quite some time.

The extensive network of outpatient facilities and inpatient centers or clinics for both men and women with substance related problems is summarized in Table 4.

TREATMENT OF ALCOHOL AND DRUG PROBLEMS

Treatment of alcohol and drug dependent persons is provided in different settings, which overlap to some extent. These include:

- outpatient facilities;
- inpatient centers and clinics;
- self-help institutions and groups;
- prisons

Outpatient Facilities

Ideally, clients with substance abuse problems enter the treatment system via outpatient facilities. If necessary, they receive counseling to motivate them to go into inpatient centers and clinics for residential treatment and rehabilitation. For aftercare, they return to their original outpatient facilities, where they see their counselors, attend self-help groups, recover and no longer need professional help. In reality, many end up in the revolving doors of the treatment system.

Outpatient facilities for clients with alcohol problems provide individual and group counseling and psychotherapy. Facilities for people with alcohol problems are set up rather traditionally with counselors waiting for their clients to come in and ask for help. In contrast, outpatient facilities for people with drug problems differ markedly in their availability and the kinds of services offered.

Outpatient facilities for drug addicts aim to guarantee survival for those who are in bad physical and mental condition, and provide opportunities for rehabilitation for those who are functioning at a higher level (Schmid et al. 2000, Simmedinger et al. 2001). In metropolitan areas, the facilities for drug addicted people offer a wide variety of services such as: fulfillment of basic needs (food, hygienic services–such as showers, washing, mending and replacing of clothes); the distribution of condoms and sterile needles; day and night shelters; injecting rooms; individual counseling and case management; medical services, including emergency treatment; methadone dispensaries; and treatment of HIV-infections and other chronic illnesses. In 1998, the City of Frankfurt has opened the first specialized institution (or hospice) for deadly ill drug addicts in order to take them off the streets and provide them with a decent place to die.

The ratio of male to female clients in outpatient facilities for alcoholics and drug addicts varies; overall, it ranges between 2:1 and 3:1. These figures include women who come to the facilities as relatives of substance dependent men. Since substance dependent women are a minority in these facilities, it is often hard for them to meet their needs. Consequently, a few agencies in metropolitan areas have opened up specialized facilities for substance dependent women. These are highly effective in reaching out to women (Schmid & Simmedinger, 2000; Vogt, 1997; Vogt & Krah, 1998).

Methadone Dispensaries

Substitution therapy is now seen as the state of the art in the medical treatment of drug addiction (Uchtenhagen, 2000). Dispensaries providing methadone or related substances, such as buprenorphine, exist alongside drug-free and other outpatient facilities for drug addicts. Data regarding how many drug addicts are on methadone or other opiate substitutes are hard to find. Overall estimates vary between 30,000 and 60,000 people (DHS, 2000, p. 149). Most are long-term addicts with a long history of treatment as well as imprisonment. Higher functioning drug addicts and those living in the countryside can obtain methadone from their family doctor.

Recently, the German federal government and the governments of several states launched a trial project to distribute prescribed heroin to a small group of opiate addicts who are in bad physical shape and do not benefit from methadone treatment (Krausz et al. 2001). This project follows standardized pharmaceutical research treatment regimes, but also integrates psychosocial care combining case management with motivational interviewing (Oliva, Gagen, Schlanstedt, Schu, & Sommer, 2001). The project is closely monitored and the results will be analyzed at the end of the trial in 2004. This is an important step that in the end will enlarge the spectrum of drugs at hand to treat opiate dependency. The usefulness of prescribing heroin to subgroups of opiate addicts has been shown in trials in Switzerland (Uchtenhagen, Dobler-Mikola, Steffen, Gutzwiller, Blättler, & Pfeifer, 2000) and in England (Farrell, Strang, Ruben, & Gossop, 1994).

Detoxification and In-Patient Treatment

Alcohol detoxification typically takes place in psychiatric wards. However, since the bulk of cases with alcohol problems are undiagnosed, detoxification is more often handled in general hospitals than in psychiatric wards (John, Hapke, Rumpf, Hill, & Dilling, 1996).

Not so for drug addicts who have to go to psychiatric wards for their detoxification. On the average, detoxification takes between 3 to 6 weeks and in recent years has included the use of short intervention techniques to encourage further treatment. Preliminary research studies show the positive effects of detoxification treatment when combined with counseling, and seems to justify the increased costs (Uchtenhagen, 2000).

The majority of residential treatment centers and specialized clinics for substance dependents take in either those who are dependent on alcohol and psychoactive medicines, or those dependent on illicit drugs. In these settings men outnumber women by 5:1 or 4:1. In less specialized institutions, such as psychiatric wards and psychosomatic clinics, which take in cases with a wide variety of mental health problems including some substance dependent patients, the male-female ratio is equal or even higher for women. Overall, the caseload of substance dependent clients in mental health settings is low, around 10% of all their patients.

The number of women in inpatient treatment centers and clinics tends to be even smaller than in outpatient settings. For instance, in a center for alcoholics with 100 patients, only 15-20% tend to be women, and in a therapeutic community with 50 drug addicts, only 10-20% are women. In such male-dominated environment, it is quite difficult for women to talk about their own problems, especially about male violence and sexual abuse. While the outcomes of women-only inpatient treatment facilities are encouraging, more research is needed (Vogt, 1998).

In the past, the length of treatment in inpatient centers and clinics was quite long. For alcoholics, treatment lasted on the average for 9 months, but was frequently expanded to 12 months, and, in a few cases, even longer. More recently, however, financial restrictions have forced the institutions to cut back, and the average treatment time for alcoholics now ranges between 3 and 4 months. For drug addicts, the average time of treatment used to be 24 months; it is now down to an average of 6 months, followed by 4 months of aftercare.

Many professionals had been concerned that shortening treatment time would have negative effects on treatment outcomes. So far, however, no data are available showing any detrimental effects as a result of reducing time in residential treatment. This may be due to the fact that the institutions had changed their treatment programs to better meet the needs of their patients.

For many years inpatient treatment was dominated by rather old-fashioned and hard-core behavior therapy concepts with crude techniques of confrontation (in group settings) and negative reinforcement. This was supplemented by the use of a hierarchy of stages that allowed clients to be promoted or degraded depending on their adherence to treatment. The treatment results were not impressive. A 1994 study (Küfner, Denis, Roch, Arzt, & Rug, 1994) showed that those treatment centers that had the best outcomes stressed relatively few rules, emphasized cooperation instead of confrontation, and provided positive reinforcement. These findings helped to start a discussion on more effective counseling approaches and elicited support for the use of motivational interviewing and cognitive behavior therapy techniques (Miller, 1999; Miller & Rollnick, 1991).

Aftercare and Self Help Programs

During the past few years, aftercare services have increased and the number of places in supervised housing projects expanded tremendously. Moreover, efforts to provide jobs for clients increased as well. In the future, the provision of after-care facilities and job training programs are high priorities in the rehabilitation of substance dependent clients.

Self help groups in Germany include Alcoholics Anonymous (AA), Narcotic Anonymous (NA), the Good Templars, as well as Junkie-Bund and JES, which are European types of self help "unions" for drug addicts that try to organize addicts into advocacy groups and to engage them in politics (see DHS, 2001). Some of them, especially AA groups and activists such as the Good Templars work hand in hand with treatment facilities. They may meet in the rooms of outpatient facilities, or have residential centers send their patients to their meetings, or invite self help speakers to lecture in treatment centers. While self-help organizations for alcoholics, such as AA and groups for their relatives have been found to be astonishingly effective (Eisenbach-Stangl & Rosenquist, 1998), this is not so for NA or the Junkie-Bund, which have been rather ineffective in mobilizing and helping drugs addicts.

Imprisonment

Approximately 10,000 to 20,000 persons–mostly men–are in prison due to drug law violation (Jacob & Stöver, 1997). Moreover, it is estimated that one third of all prison inmates are users of psychoactive substances and one third of them have been drug dependent long before going to jail. While in jail, their drug problems tend to get worse because of lack of treatment on the one hand (see Kalinowski & Schaper, 1997) and the ready availability of licit and illicit drugs that are smuggled into prisons, on the other hand. In the majority of cases, the overall effects of imprisonment are negative. Only in a few cases are individuals able to manage to detoxify themselves in prison, get off drugs and profit from social work programs.

THE ROLE OF SOCIAL WORKERS

Social workers have been part of the German alcohol treatment system since its beginnings around 1900. They helped get men in need of treatment into institutions, worked with them during it, and cared for them afterwards. While the treatment underwent dramatic changes during the last century, social workers stayed on and changed their role as well (Schmid & Vogt, 2001).

Currently, social workers are found in both the outpatient and in-patient facilities for alcoholic and drug dependent individuals. An estimated 70% of those working in outpatient counseling facilities are trained as social workers or social educators, and the outpatient segment of the treatment system is dominated by social work concepts (cf. Stöver, 1999). However, things are changing as more and more doctors and psychologists are being hired, especially in facilities for drug dependents. This may influence the organization of services and eventually enhance existing counseling concepts (Schu, Schmid, Gagen,, Vogt, & Oliva, 2002) by stressing the focus on the motivation of clients, and including more cognitive behavior modification techniques and combining it with medical treatment, such as anti-craving medications (Goez, 1999). So far, only a minority of social workers is trained in these new approaches. If they want to dominate the field in the future, they will need to improve their knowledge and skills in these new approaches.

In inpatient centers and clinics, only 30% of the staff are trained as social workers or social educators, and nearly all of them have some additional training in psychotherapy. Part of their work can be described as case management, linking clients with institutions outside the treatment center, helping them to get prepared to return home after 3 to 6 months of treatment, and, if necessary, helping them to reorganize their lives. Often, social workers also provide direct treatment, especially in group sessions where they work closely together with psychotherapists. The influence of social workers, however, on treatment concepts and procedures is rather marginal and there are no indications that this will change in the future.

Social Work and Research

The role of social workers in research has changed over the years. In the 1970s and 80s, few social workers were involved in research projects on substance dependencies. This has changed in the last 10 years as social workers assumed greater role in this area. Currently, the main areas of research are: (1) consumption patterns, epidemiology and development of models to estimate prevalence rates; (2) youth and risk behavior (for alcohol and drug use and abuse), including prevention and management of risk behavior and life-skills-trainings; (3) impact of growing up in families with substance dependents, and identifying risk and protective factors in adult children of substance dependents; (4) ecstasy, cocaine and crack and its effects; (5) gender differences in consumption patterns, risk behavior and protective factors, as well as in the lifestyles of substance dependents; (6) effects of different methods of counseling and treatment (including the use of medications), relapse prevention, and harm reduction measures in outpatient facilities and in prison.

With increasing interest of social workers in research, social work as a profession is itself changing, becoming more professional and more diversified. This further stimulates research about the profession itself, the work places of social workers, and their skills as treatment providers.

CONCLUSION

In the last 30 years, substance use and abuse problems changed dramatically in Germany and with it the role of social work in prevention, treatment, aftercare and research. In fact, social workers developed their own concepts in dealing with alcohol and drug addicts, stressing harm reduction measures and the establishment of "low-threshold" institutions that offer easy accessibility to meet basic survival needs, such as the availability of day and night shelters. These have evolved into more complex centers integrating a wide variety of services including professional counseling and outpatient psychotherapy, and medical services. However, times are changing and with them the need to revise social work training based on research findings on what works in primary prevention, treatment and rehabilitation of clients with alcohol and drug problems.

REFERENCES

DHS (Ed.) (1997). *Jahrbuch Sucht 1998.* Geesthacht: Neuland
DHS (Ed.) (2000). *Jahrbuch Sucht 2001.* Geesthacht: Neuland
DHS (Ed.) (2001). *Jahrbuch Sucht 2002* (pp. 231-233) Geesthacht: Neuland
Eisenbach-Stangl, I. & Rosenqvist, P. (Eds.) (1998). *Diversity in Unity: Studies on Alcoholics Anonymous in eight societies.* NAD-publication 33. Helsinki
Farrell, M., Strang, J., Ruben, S. & Gossop, M. (Eds.) (1994). *Heroin addiction and drug policy.* New York: Oxford University Press
Frieg, K. & Lipp, U. (2001). *Substanzkonsum von psychotropen Drogen von Studierenden der Fachhochschule Frankfurt am Main.* Frankfurt: Diplomarbeit am Fachbereich Sozialarbeit (unpublished)
Goez, J. (Ed.) (1999). *Der drogenabhaegige Patient.* Moechen: Urban & Fischer
Hüllinghorst, R. (2000). Präventive Sucht- und Drogenpolitik in der Bundesrepublik Deutschland. In Schmidt, B. & Hurrelmann, K. (Eds.). *Präventive Sucht-und Drogenpolitik,* pp. 267-282. Opladen: Leske & Budrich
Jacob, J. & Stöver, H. (1997): *Drogen und Drogengebraucherinnen im Strafvollzug.* In Jacob, J., Keppler, K. & Stöver, H. (Eds.), *Drogengebrauch und Infektionsgeschehen (HIV/AIDS und Hepatitis) im Strafvollzug* pp.17-30. Berlin: Deutsche AIDS-Hilfe
John, U., Hapke, U., Rumpf, H.-J., Hill, A. & Dilling, H. (1996). *Prävalenz und Sekundärprävention von Alkoholmissbrauch und-abhängigkeit in der medizinischen Versorgung.* Baden-Baden: Nomos
Kalinowski, H. & Schaper, G. (1997): *Vollzugsinterne medizinische und psychosoziale Hilfen für drogengebrauchende Gefangene.* In Jacob, J., Keppler, K. & Stöver, H. (eds.): *Drogengebrauch und Infektionsgeschehen (HIV/AIDS und Hepatitis) im Strafvollzug* pp. 61-72. Berlin: Deutsche AIDS-Hilfe
Kleiber, D. & Soellner, R. (1998). *Cannabiskonsum.* Weinheim: Juventa
Kraus, L. & Augustin, R. (2001): Repräsentativerhebung zum Gebrauch psychoaktiver Substanzen bei Erwachsenen in Deutschland 2000. *Sucht,* 47, Sonderheft 1
Kraus, L. & Bauernfeind, R. (1998). Repräsentativerhebung zum Gebrauch psychoaktiver Substanzen bei Erwachsenen in Deutschland 1997. *Sucht,* 44, Sonderheft 1
Krausz, M. et al. (2001). *Das bundesdeutsche Modellprojekt zur heroingestoeten Behandlung Opiatabhoegiger-eine multizentrische, randomisierte, kontrollierte Therapiestudie.* Hamburg (not published)
Krausz, M. & Raschke, P. (Eds.) (1999): *Drogen in der Metropole.* Freiburg: Lambertus
Küfner, H., Denis, A., Roch,I., Arzt, J. & Rug, U. (1994). *Stationäre Krisenintervention bei Drogenabhängigen.* Baden-Baden: Nomos
Martius, W. (1908). *Deutsche Trinkerheilstätten.* Berlin: Mässigkeits-Verlag
Maschewsky-Schneider, U. (1997). *Frauen sind anders krank.* Weinheim: Juventa
Miller, W. R. (1999). Enhancing motivation for change in substance abuse treatment. *Treatment Improvement Protocol (TIP),* Series 35. Rockville: CSAT

Miller, W. R. & Rollnick, S. (1991). Motivational Interviewing. New York: Guilford

Oliva, H., Gagen, W., Schlanstedt, G., Schu, M. & Sommer, L. (2001). *Case Management in der Suchtkranken-und Drogenhilfe*. Baden-Baden: Nomos

Röhrle, B. & Sommer, G. (Eds.) (1999). *Prävention und Gesundheitsförderung*. Tübingen: DGVT

Schmid, M. & Simmedinger, R. (2000). *Gibt es eine Zukunft nach der Therapie?* Frankfurt: ISS

Schmid, M., Simmedinger, R. & Vogt, I. (2000). Ambulante Suchthilfe in Hamburg. *Statusbericht 1999*. Frankfurt: ISS

Schmid, M. & Vogt, I. (2001). Case Management und Motivierende Beratung im Rahmen des Modellversuchs zur opiatgestützten Behandlung. *Suchttherapie, 2*, 73-79

Schmidt, B. & Hurrelmann, K. (Eds.) (2000). *Präventive Sucht-und Drogenpolitik*. Opladen: Leske & Budrich

Schu, M., Schmid, M. Görgen, W. Vogt, I. & Oliva, H. (2002). *Case Management und Motivational Interviewing Manual*. Weinheim: Beltz.

Simmedinger, R., Schmid, M. & Vogt, I. (2001). *Ambulante Suchthilfe in Hamburg. Statusbericht 2000*. Frankfurt: ISS

Soellner, R. (2000). *Abhängig von Haschisch?* Bern: Huber

Stöver, H. (Ed.)(1999). *Akzeptierende Drogenarbeit*. Freiburg: Lambertus

Uchtenhagen, A. (2000). Substitutionsbehandlung. In Uchtenhagen, A. & Zieglgängsberger, W. (Eds.): *Suchtmedizin*, (pp. 353-364). München: Urban & Fischer

Uchtenhagen, A., Dobler-Mikola, A., Steffen, T., Gutzwiller, F., Blättler, R. & Pfeifer, S. (2000). *Betäubungsmittelverschreibung an Heroinabhängige*. Basel: Karger

Vogt, I. (1994). *Alkoholikerinnen*. Freiburg: Lambertus

Vogt, I. (1997). Bella Donna. *Die Frauendrogenberatungsstelle im Ruhrgebiet*. Berlin: VWB

Vogt, I. (1998). Gender and drug treatment systems. In Klingemann, H. & Hunt, G. (Eds.): *Drug treatment systems in an international perspective* (pp. 281-297). Thousand Oaks, CA: Sage

Vogt, I. (2000). Gender differences in help-seeking behavior of heroin users in Germany. In: Springer, A. & Uhl, A. (Eds.) *Illicit drugs* (pp.261-274). Innsbruck: StudienVerlag,

Vogt, I. & Krah, K. (1998). Klientinnen beurteilen Frauenhilfeeinrichtungen. In: Akzept & Trimbos-Institut (Eds.) *The times, they are a-changin'* (pp. 97-110). Berlin: VWB

Vogt. I., Leopold, B., Tödte, M. & Breuker-Gerbig, U. (1998). Frauen und Sucht. Düsseldorf: Ministerium für Frauen, Jugend, Familie und Gesundheit des Landes Nordrhein-Westfalen

Vogt, I. & Schmid, M. (1998). Illicit drugs in Germany and the emergence of the modern drug treatment system. In: Klingemann, H. & Hunt, G. (Eds.): *Drug treatment systems in an international perspective* (pp. 145-157). Thousand Oaks, CA: Sage

Vogt, I. & Schmid, M. (2000): Crack-Konsum in der Drogenszene in Frankfurt am Main: Ergebnisse empirischer Studien. *Wiener Zeitschrift für Suchtforschung*, 23, 5-13

WHO (1986). *Ottawa Charta zur Gesundheitsf_derung*. Genf: WHO

Social Work and the Treatment
of Substance Abuse in Israel

Neta Peleg-Oren
Giora Rahav
Meir Teichman

SUMMARY. This paper examines the role of the social worker within the field of substance abuse in Israel at the start of the 21st century, its implications for the profession, and the training of its practitioners. Addiction to psychoactive substances is viewed as a bio-psycho-social phenomenon caused by a wide variety of factors and the respective interactions between them, placing it within the realm of the expertise of the social worker. The social worker plays a central role in providing both administrative and clinical interventions with this population. Additional ways in which the education and training of social workers can prepare them to deal more efficiently and comprehensively with the problem of substance abuse in both practical and academic terms is discussed. *[Article copies available for a fee from The Haworth Document Delivery Service: 1-800-HAWORTH. E-mail address: <getinfo@haworthpressinc.com> Website: <http://www.HaworthPress.com> © 2002 by The Haworth Press, Inc. All rights reserved.]*

Neta Peleg-Oren, PhD, is Lecturer, Bar Ilan University School of Social Work, Giora Rahav, PhD, is Professor, Department of Sociology and the Bob Shapell School of Social Work, Tel Aviv University, and Meir Teichman, PhD, is Professor and Head of the Bob Shapell School of Social Work, Tel-Aviv University, Israel.

Address correspondence to: Dr. Meir Teichman, Tel-Aviv University, Bob Shapell School of Social Work, Tel-Aviv 69978, Israel (E-mail: teichma@ post.tau.ac.il).

[Haworth co-indexing entry note]: "Social Work and the Treatment of Substance Abuse in Israel." Peleg-Oren, Neta, Giora Rahav, and Meir Teichman. Co-published simultaneously in *Journal of Social Work Practice in the Addictions* (The Haworth Social Work Practice Press, an imprint of The Haworth Press, Inc.) Vol. 2, No. 3/4, 2002, pp. 85-96; and: *International Aspects of Social Work Practice in the Addictions* (ed: Shulamith Lala Ashenberg Straussner, and Larry Harrison) The Haworth Social Work Practice Press, an imprint of The Haworth Press, Inc., 2002, pp. 85-96. Single or multiple copies of this article are available for a fee from The Haworth Document Delivery Service [1-800-HAWORTH, 9:00 a.m. - 5:00 p.m. (EST). E-mail address: getinfo@haworthpressinc.com].

KEYWORDS. Treatment of addictions in Israel, social work profession, policy, prevention

INTRODUCTION

The start of the 21st century seems an appropriate time to survey the phenomenon of substance abuse in Israel and the existing system of interventions in addictions. What is of particular interest is the significance and implications of this problem for social work in terms of policy, research, and practice.

The 1990s saw a rise in the total consumption of alcohol and other psychoactive substances in the Israeli population. During this period, the country also underwent considerable demographic and social change in the wake of the arrival of hundreds of thousands of immigrants from the former Soviet Union and Ethiopia, along with the entrance of two to three hundred thousand foreign workers into the economy. It is reasonable to assume that this immigration played a significant role in the increase in the consumption of alcohol and other psychoactive substances.

Immigration is often associated with severe distress caused by the economical hardship and the difficulties of social adjustment to a different culture. In addition, the fact that heavy alcohol consumption is part of the lifestyle in the Former Soviet Union and other countries in Eastern Europe seems to provide an additional connection between immigration to Israel in the 1990s and the escalation in the consumption of alcohol, and even other drugs (Barnea & Teichman, 1993; Rahav, Teichman, Gil, Rosenbloom, & Bar-Hamburger, 1998).

Another unique feature of Israeli society that also has implications for substance abuse and addiction is the fact that it is divided primarily into two distinct cultural groups: Jews, accounting for some 80% of the Israeli population; and Arabs (most of them Moslems) constituting the remaining 20%. Judaism and Islam relate differentially to the use of alcohol and other drugs. Islam mandates a total ban on alcoholic beverages and other intoxicants; nevertheless, the use of hashish is endemic to the Middle East. In contrast, the Jewish tradition acknowledges both the advantages and disadvantages of alcohol consumption. Drinking of wine is part of every religious ritual (Straussner, 2001a). Although Judaism does not relate specifically to other drugs, it takes an emphatically negative stance toward substance abuse and the ensuing loss of control. The influence of these complex cultural traditions (Jewish and

Muslim) has been the subject of several studies on the use of drugs and alcohol in Israel (e.g., Neumark, Rahav, & Teichman, 2001; Rahav & Teichman, in press; Teichman, Rahav, & Barnea, 1994).

SCOPE OF ALCOHOL AND DRUG PROBLEMS

No reliable official statistics are available regarding the number of people addicted to psychoactive substances in Israel. Toward the end of the 20th century, estimates put the figures of Jewish substance abusers at between 50,000 and 100,000 alcoholics (0.8%-1.5% of the total population), and between 14,000 and 30,000 drug addicted people (0.2%-0.5% of the total population) (Amram & Ya'akov, 2000; Weiss, 2000). These figures do not distinguish between those who are addicted/dependent or abusing a substance. Therefore, the wide range represented by these figures stems, as in other countries (see, Straussner, 1993; Teichman, 2001), from the use of different definitions of dependency and abuse, as well as different methods for estimating the extent of the phenomenon. Moreover, the particular traits of the population involved, and the fact that substance abusers are reluctant to declare themselves openly, makes it difficult to produce accurate figures.

Exploratory studies of drug abusers registered with the Israeli social welfare agencies and health authorities reveal that they experience severe economic, social, and emotional distress, and many are engaged in criminal activity (Amram & Ya'akov, 2000). Furthermore, the majority of addicted people registered with the social security and welfare agencies are males between the ages of 25 and 40, predominantly single, divorced, or separated. Most of them were born in Israel, are of Jewish Middle East/North African origin, come from large families, and their substance abuse began when they were in their teens (Amram & Ya'akov, 2000). During the 1990s, studies of heroin-addicted immigrants from Former Soviet Unions in the Southern region of Israel indicated that approximately one-third of them were not Jewish (Isralowitz, 2001).

The population of alcoholics also consists primarily of males, but is generally older, with the average age of 40 years. Most are married and unemployed. Unlike the population of drug addicts, only one-third of the alcoholics were born in Israel, the rest come from Eastern Europe or Middle East/North Africa. The majority of this population have an elementary or incomplete high school education. Since the mid-1990s, there has been a rise in the number of alcoholics with a high school, or even higher education; many of them are immigrants from the various former Soviet Union countries (Michaeli, 1992; The Association for the Prevention of Alcoholism, 2000).

The treatment of addictions in Israel involves a range of professions, including medicine, psychology, criminology, and social work (Barnea & Teichman, 1993). Although law enforcement and medical approaches are still prevalent in Israel, substance abuse is increasingly viewed as a social problem. There is considerable public awareness of the seriousness of substance use and addiction, and the magnitude of its effects upon the society as a whole, and in particular on the individuals associated with the addict or alcoholic. As a result, a growing number of legal and therapeutic services are being established to limit supply and demand, and to reduce the harm caused by the use of psychoactive substances.

ROLE OF THE SOCIAL WORK PROFESSION

Social work is increasingly becoming a pivotal profession in the field of substance abuse, playing a major role in the shaping and implementation of social policies. In this respect, the situation in Israel differs from what is common in many other Western countries (Roiblatt & Dinis, 2001; Straussner, 2001b). The following discussion will describe the contribution of social work in Israel to challenging the problem of drug and alcohol abuse in terms of social policy, treatment and rehabilitation, and education and training.

Contribution to Social Policy

As part of the national efforts to struggle with substance abuse in Israel, a national authority was set up. It is a statutory body that functions under the National Anti-Drug Authority (ADA) Law of 1988. Its major role is to form national social policies for prevention, treatment, rehabilitation, punishment and law enforcement. It also coordinates among the government ministries and agencies that deal with substance abuse and supports basic and applied research in this area. These policies serve as the basis for activities of the national as well as local authorities with respect to substance use, abuse and addictions. As such, it is not an executive body, but rather initiates, advises, and coordinates among the government ministries, the local authorities, and other institutions or organizations active in the domain of substance use and abuse.

The establishment of the Anti-Drug Authority (ADA) provided an impetus in the treatment of the social problem of drug and alcohol abuse and spurred growth in the number of treatment settings and admission slots. Nonetheless, the number, variety, and size of the different programs still appear insufficient to provide a comprehensive response to the need for treatment and rehabilitation.

Social work plays a dominant role in shaping the ADA's policies on treatment, rehabilitation, and prevention. This can be attributed to the fact that the study of substance abuse is included in the basic training of social workers in Israel, who in turn, view this area of activity as an integral part of their work. Furthermore, Israeli welfare policy dealing with addiction, entrust social workers to facilitate implementation. For instance, the Social Security Institute fulfills a crucial social policy function by providing substance abusers with monthly disability remuneration. The social worker is required to submit a monthly report on the condition of the addict, and to inform the Institute of Social Security about the conclusion or cessation of treatment (Ministry of Social Welfare, Directives and Regulations, 2000).

Contribution to Treatment and Rehabilitation

Social work is represented in the three sectors dealing with treatment and rehabilitation of people addicted to alcoholic beverages and psychoactive substances: Government and public bodies directly involved in the treatment of the client and his or her family; non-government organizations (NGOs) such as AA, NA, the Association of Family Members of Substance Abusers, etc.; and the private enterprises established by social workers, mainly in collaboration with other professionals such as psychiatrists and clinical psychologists, to provide counseling and treatment (the latter sector is not reviewed in this paper). It is important to note here that the National Health Law, enacted in Israel in 1990, does not cover the treatment of substance abuse and addictions among the services provided by the national health services. This fact has major financial and social implications for the public or governmental organizations involved in such treatment, as well as for the growing number of NGOs in the field. Moreover, it is interesting to note that even among the programs that are described below and that are supported by government funds, almost no follow-up and evaluation studies have been carried out.

Drug detoxification and follow-up treatment: Detoxification from drugs is carried out in six adult and one adolescent inpatient units and seven ambulatory centers. All of them utilize a combination of physical detoxification and psychosocial therapies. These units serve as the first stage in the treatment and rehabilitation process and are managed jointly by the Ministry of Health and the Ministry of Social Welfare.

In addition, sixteen community day centers for drug addicts operate throughout Israel. They are financed jointly by the Ministry of Social Welfare, the local authorities, and the ADA (Report of the Ministry of Social Welfare, 2000). These centers offer various services ranging from early detection of alcohol and drug related problems, diagnosis and referral of addicts in their area, to detoxification units and subsequent ongoing psychosocial therapies, mainly on an individual basis. At a later stage in the rehabilitation process, drug abusers are reassigned to these community centers for ongoing treatment and care. At these community day-centers, they participate in various rehabilitative programs designed to help them establish a normative daily schedule, learn limit-setting and self-control, and receive training aimed at re-entering the job market. As a rule, the community day centers treat individuals who have already undergone drug detoxification, and who require further psychosocial therapy and follow-up. However, these centers also serve as screening facilities that evaluate addicted persons for either in-home detoxification or admission to detoxification units (Ben-David-Gerasi, 1995). According to the Ministry of Social Welfare reports, during the year 1999, about 5,000 adult drug abusers were treated in community day centers. On the average, they spend about eighteen months in any of the day centers.

Social workers play a dominant role in the drug detoxification units and community centers. In most settings social workers serve as administrators as well as clinical practitioners with special expertise in working with addictions. Physicians act as providers and consultants of psychiatric and medical services.

Alcohol detoxification and follow-up treatment: Unlike detoxification from drugs, detoxification for alcohol dependence comes under the auspices of the Israeli Society for the Prevention of Alcoholism and is affiliated with the Ministry of Health. There is only one alcohol inpatient treatment unit in Israel. It was established in 1982 and contains 30 beds. The ambulatory system for alcoholics is managed in part by an NGO and in part by the local authorities. The major organization is *Efshar* ("It's Possible" in Hebrew). It is a NGO set up for the specific purpose of operating social services for people with alcohol problems and is funded primarily by the government. This organization, founded in 1986, maintains seven day-centers and three branches. Eight additional day-centers were established and are run by the local authorities. All are headed by social workers that are in charge of a team of social workers, clinical psychologists, and counselors. The Ministry of Social Welfare finances these centers (Michaeli & Ashkenazi, 1992).

Detoxification and rehabilitation in the prisons: The Israeli prison authority has established a drug detoxification and rehabilitation unit in almost every prison. In addition, one prison was converted exclusively into a treatment and rehabilitation facility for addicted prisoners. Multi-disciplinary teams staff these units, and the ensuing treatment is conducted primarily by social workers.

Methadone maintenance programs: Ten methadone maintenance day-center programs operate in Israel. Their short-term goals include: preventing, and/or reducing the damage caused by narcotic addiction, curbing criminal activity associated with drug abuse, and relieving the addict from the cycle of infectious diseases. In the long-term, these centers aim to promote the drug abuser's personal health, family relationships, and occupational rehabilitation. Unlike other community day-centers, a psychiatrist or a physician head the methadone clinics (as stipulated by the Israeli law). However, the staff of the methadone centers always includes social workers, psychologists or therapists, nurses, and counselors.

Therapeutic communities and hostels: Several NGOs have set up drug-free therapeutic communities for drug abusers, which are funded by the Ministry of Social Welfare and the ADA. However, no therapeutic community for alcoholics exists in Israel. In 1999, about 500 drug-addicted persons were treated at eight therapeutic communities (Report of the Ministry of Social Welfare, 2000).

The Ministry of Social Welfare also manages two hostels. The first hostel, in Jerusalem, was established in 1990 and hosts twelve residents. The other, "a warm home" in the central region of the country, was opened in 1994 and hosts thirteen residents. This hostel is reserved primarily for homeless alcoholics. The hostels provide their residents with living quarters and assistance in finding employment as part of an overall rehabilitation program. In both the therapeutic communities and hostels social workers play a dominant role.

A third hostel, a joint venture of the Prisoners Rehabilitation Authority (the Ministry of Social Welfare) and a NGO, serves primarily released prisoners in the central region of the country. Most of its residents, however, are recovering drug addicts.

- *Occupational rehabilitation*: Several of the day centers have an on-site experimental "technological preparatory school." These experimental programs served only recovering substance abusers who are offered the opportunity to complete up to ten years of schooling, in addition to vocational training. At the present time, there are six such programs, all under the auspices and supervision of the Ministry of Social Welfare (Report of the Ministry of Labor and Social Welfare, 2000).
- *Non-Government Organizations (NGOs)*: Besides programs that were initiated by NGOs but are financed by the government, three different voluntary groups initiated and established various self-help groups and small therapeutic community programs for substance abusers in Israel. The first one includes members of Alcoholic Anonymous (AA) and Narcotic Anonymous (NA) groups; the second group consists of family members, parents in particular, who took the initiative to help their offspring; and the third group is comprised of various professionals such as social workers, clinical psychologists, lawyers, etc., who are concerned about various social issues, and addictions in particular, and assumed the role of community activists.

The NGOs associated with the first group (self-help organizations like AA and NA) deal with the substance abusers themselves or provide support and assistance to their families. Although run primarily by their own members, several of these organizations are aided by social workers. Those NGOs that were established by professionals defined their role as raising public awareness and initiating community action and government involvement in the prevention and treatment of substance abuse problems. These groups, in particular the Al-Sam ("No Drug" in Hebrew) Association, set up the first drug rehabilitation program and methadone maintenance clinic in Israel, the first walk-in-clinic for adolescents, and helped to establish the first professionally run therapeutic community.

Education and Training

The training of professionals to challenge substance abuse issues is offered by the central school of the Ministry of Welfare. The program provides the students with theoretical and applied knowledge ranging from general information about the etiology and factors affecting the various psychoactive substances and their use, through the variety of applicable intervention methods. Furthermore, the regulations and directives of the Ministry of Social Welfare (March, 2000) require social workers wishing to treat drug abusers and their families, to take a one-year basic training course in the subject as a prerequisite for employment. In addition, ongoing training and supervision are required of all personnel, social workers included, employed in the field of addictions. A two-year community college program that offers counselor training to recovering alcoholics and drug abusers has, for the past five years, served as a vehicle for several graduates to enroll in further education at a school of social work.

Currently, an introductory course in psychoactive substance use and addictions is offered at every university and college in the country. Nevertheless, no full academic program specializing in addictions has been instituted as yet, although a graduate MA program in social work specializing in addictions had been previously offered at Tel-Aviv University. Nevertheless, it is worth noting that most of the senior researchers in the social and behavioral sciences in Israel who are involved in the field of substance abuse are on the faculty of schools of social work.

The increase in the number of social workers wishing to become involved in the treatment of addictions has led to a growing demand for relevant in-service training programs. In response, several universities now provide such training to licensed social workers as part of their continuing education programs. The Ministry of Social Welfare also offers a one-year training course for social workers newly hired by treatment and rehabilitation centers.

IMPLICATION FOR SOCIAL WORK

The involvement of social work in the field of substance abuse and addictions is now undergoing marked change in terms of both professionalism and training. The most prominent development is the ongoing process of specialization. The Israeli Union of Social Workers is currently setting up a division of members engaged in the treatment of substance abuse and addictions with the aim of bringing together all social workers involved in the field, whether directly or indirectly, so that they can work to promote professionalism and establish licensing criteria. The division will also gather information, expand the system of professional in-service training, and serve as a lobby to consolidate the role of social work in the field of substance abuse and addictions.

The second change is introducing addictions to the academic and research community in order to upgrade the profession. As previously noted, academic professional training opportunities are still insignificant and are largely provided through the non-academic auspices of the Ministry of Social Welfare and the ADA. Nevertheless, the schools of social work are now considering the possibility of extending their training programs in several directions including:

1. Incorporating the study of addiction as a systematic and integral part of the B.S.W., M.S.W, and Ph.D. degrees curricula in social work.
2. Developing continuing education programs designed for practicing social workers in the field, as well as for non-professionals, such as addiction counselors.
3. Continuing to provide field training for social work students in treatment centers for drug and alcohol abuse, although this training is not fully integrated into the advanced programs in social work.
4. Establishing a network of academic research centers for the study of substance abuse and addictions to be allied with the schools of social work and treatment centers. Such arrangements would be mutually beneficial, with the field gaining from academic knowledge, and the university gaining from exposure to the problems and changes in the field. It would be important for these centers to focus on theoretical and practical elements (e.g., the causes of drug and alcohol abuse, the population at risk, epidemiology, different treatment approaches, techniques and models, education and prevention), and research components (e.g., theoretical and basic research, program evaluation, epidemiological research, development of new intervention models, etc.).

CONCLUSION

At the beginning of the third millennium, the system of treatment and rehabilitation of alcohol and drug dependent persons is comprised of a wide range of programs administered by the Ministry of Social Welfare, the Ministry of Health, the Prison Service, the Anti-Drug Authority, and various NGOs. Nevertheless, the formation of a comprehensive national social policy is still underway, and despite the progress that has been made, it remains difficult to discern a clear policy of treatment and rehabilitation for substance abuser and addicts in Israel (Rahav, 2000). The nature of the coordination between the different government ministries (health, social welfare, education, justice and law enforcement) and non-governmental organizations of various types that are involved in this effort is not always explicitly defined. This state of affairs tends to make the efficient operation of existing treatment settings and facilities somewhat cumbersome. Obstacles to treatment and prevention programs continue to exist, particularly since the Israeli National Health Law does not relate specifically to substance abuse, and does not cover the cost of the treatment of addictions.

To sum up, the profession of social work in Israel has contributed considerably to the expansion of substance abuse knowledge and should aspire to continue to play a leading role in advocating for humane public policy formation and better coordination of substance abuse treatment services.

REFERENCES

Amram, Y., & Ya'akov, B. (2000). *The estimation and condition of drug addicts in Israel*. Jerusalem, Israel: The Hebrew University (Unpublished manuscript).

Anti-Drug Authority. (No date). *The treatment and rehabilitation of drug abusers*. Jerusalem, Israel: Electronic source: <*www.antidrugs.org.il*>.

Barnea, Z., & Teichman, M. (1993). Alcohol and drug abuse in Israel in the twenty-first century: Implications for social work education. *International Social Work, 36:* 357-372.

Ben-David-Gerasi, N. (1995). *The struggle with drugs: Changing to municipal organizing in Tel-Aviv City*. Jerusalem, Israel: Unpublished master thesis, The Hebrew University (Hebrew).

Efshar. (No date). *Unit for the treatment of victims of alcohol*. Ramat-Gan, Israel: Electronic source: <*www.efshar.org.il*>.

Israeli Society for the Prevention of Alcoholism. (No date). *Prevention and treatment of alcoholics*. Ramat-Gan, Israel: Electronic source: <*www.ias.org.uk/ispa*>.

Isralowitz, R.E. (2001). Toward an understanding of Russian speaking heroin addicts and drug treatment services in Israel. *Journal of Social Work Practice in the Addictions,* 1(2): 33-44.

Michaeli, N. (1992). The profile of the Israeli addict. *Mifgash–A Journal of Educational Social Work, 3:* 117-127, (Hebrew).

Michaeli, N., & Ashkenazi, S. (1992). *The Unit for Treatment Alcohol Addicts*. Jerusalem, Israel: Efshar, Ministry of Social Welfare (Hebrew).

Ministry of Health, Ministry of Welfare, & Anti-Drug Authority. (1994). *Guideline of treatment facilities for substance abusers*. Jerusalem, Israel: The Department of Addictions, (Hebrew).

Ministry of Social Welfare, (2000). *Instruction number 27, chapter 3.* Jerusalem, Israel: The Department of Addictions (Hebrew).

Ministry of Social Welfare. (2000). *Yearly report.* Jerusalem, Israel: The Department of Addictions (Hebrew).

Neumark, Y., Rahav, G., Teichman, M., & Hassin, D. (2001). Alcohol drinking patterns among Jewish and Arab men and women in Israel. *Journal of Studies on Alcohol, 62,* 443-447.

Rahav, G. (2000). *The drug market in the greater Tel-Aviv area: Report submitted to UNICRI.* Tel Aviv, Israel: Tel-Aviv University, The Institute for Social Research, (Hebrew).

Rahav, G., & Teichman, M. (2002). Epidemiological Examination of Patterns of Drug Use in Israel. In R. Isralowitz, M. Afifi & R. Rawson (Eds.), *Drug Addiction Policy and Program Development: Middle-East People in Transition.* Los Angeles, CA: Praeger.

Rahav, G., Teichman, M., Gil, R., Rosenbloom, Y., & Bar-Hamburger, R. (1998). *The use of psychoactive substances in Israel: The 4th epidemiological study.* Jerusalem, Israel: ADA (Hebrew).

Roiblatt, R.E., & Dinis, M.C. (2001). *The lost link: Social work pioneers in the early 20th century alcohol policy.* Paper presented at the KBS Alcohol Epidemiology Symposium. Toronto, Canada.

Straussner, S.L.A. (1993). "Assessment and Treatment of Clients with Alcohol and Other Drug Abuse Problems: An Overview" in Straussner, S. L.A. (Ed.). *Clinical Work with Substance Abusing Clients* (pp 3-30). New York: Guilford Press.

Straussner, S.L.A. (2001a) Jewish substance abusers: Existing, but invisible. In Straussner, S.L.A. (Ed). *Ethnocultural Factors in the Treatment of Addictions.* (pp. 291-317). New York: Guilford.

Straussner, S.L.A (2001b). The role of social workers in the treatment of addictions: A brief history. *Journal of Social Work Practice in the Addictions,* 1(1): 3-9.

Teichman, M., Rahav, G., & Barnea, Z. (1994). Alcohol Consumption among Non-Jewish Men in Israel. *Alcologia: European Journal of Alcohol Studies, 6:* 201-206.

Teichman, M. (2001). *Alcohol and alcoholism: Causes, prevention, and treatment.* Tel-Aviv: Ramot, Tel-Aviv University (Hebrew).

Weiss, S. (2000). The treatment needs of addiction to alcohol in Israel and the research in the alcohol implication in the beginning of the third millenium. *Harefuah, 2:* 550-552 (Hebrew).

Weiss, S., Sawa, S., Abdeen, Z., & Yanai, J. (1999). Substance abuse studies and prevention efforts among Arabs in the 1990s in Israel, Jordan and the Palestinian Authority: A literature review. *Addiction, 94:* 177-198.

Drug and Alcohol Addiction in Singapore: Issues and Challenges in Control and Treatment Strategies

Mohd Maliki Osman

SUMMARY. The problem of drug addiction in Singapore has been relatively under control over the past few years. This is a result of the strategy of controlling supply to reduce demand for drugs. Alcohol consumption in Singapore is relatively low compared to Western countries. This paper provides an overview of the drug and alcohol control and treatment strategies adopted in Singapore. While new strategies have been formulated, some issues and challenges still remain. These issues and challenges are discussed and findings of a recent study conducted by the author are described. They include the need to focus on gateway drugs like alcohol, intervention involving family members, opportunities for regular employment for drug addicts, and the role of religion in aftercare treatment. *[Article copies available for a fee from The Haworth Document Delivery Service: 1-800-HAWORTH. E-mail address: <getinfo@haworthpressinc.com> Website: <http://www.HaworthPress.com> © 2002 by The Haworth Press, Inc. All rights reserved.]*

KEYWORDS. Drug and alcohol use in Singapore, addiction, treatment, challenges, role of religion

---

Mohd Maliki Osman is on the faculty of the National University of Singapore.

[Haworth co-indexing entry note]: "Drug and Alcohol Addiction in Singapore: Issues and Challenges in Control and Treatment Strategies." Osman, Mohd Maliki. Co-published simultaneously in *Journal of Social Work Practice in the Addictions* (The Haworth Social Work Practice Press, an imprint of The Haworth Press, Inc.) Vol. 2, No. 3/4, 2002, pp. 97-117; and: *International Aspects of Social Work Practice in the Addictions* (ed: Shulamith Lala Ashenberg Straussner, and Larry Harrison) The Haworth Social Work Practice Press, an imprint of The Haworth Press, Inc., 2002, pp. 97-117. Single or multiple copies of this article are available for a fee from The Haworth Document Delivery Service [1-800-HAWORTH, 9:00 a.m. - 5:00 p.m. (EST). E-mail address: getinfo@haworthpressinc.com].

INTRODUCTION

For more than two decades, the government of Singapore has been battling the war on drugs. The problem of drug abuse has taken many forms. It has moved from the sudden surge of heroin addiction in the 1970s, to inhalant abuse in the mid 1980s by young people, and to the emergence of designer drugs like "ice" (methaphetamine hydrochloride) and "ecstasy" (methylenediocy-methamphetamine) in the 1990s. Drug laws in Singapore have been regarded as one of the strictest in the world. These laws have helped to control the abuse of drugs (National Council Against Drug Abuse, 1998).

The current economic crisis facing the region is a crucial context in reviewing the efforts taken at fighting the drug war. Singapore, along with other countries in Southeast Asia, was hit hard during the Asian financial crises in 1998. Currently, Singapore is reported to be undergoing a technical economic recession. Millions of dollars has been spent on combating the problem of drug abuse and millions of dollars more has been spent by the abusers in supporting their habits. Estimates noted that in Singapore, drug addicts spend at least $35 million a year on dangerous drugs ("They spend," 1998). According to the Central Narcotics Bureau (CNB), a new drug abuser spends about $7,500 a year on drugs, while a hardcore heroin addict spends an average of $37,000 per year on drugs ("They spend," 1998). Governmental expenditures on drug control and treatment programs have been equally high, with the government spending more than $40 million a year (National Council Against Drug Abuse, 1998). These addicts are important human resources. The manpower cost lost due to their drug addiction has not been estimated. In times of scarce resources and in the context of a gloomy economic forecast for the region, Singapore is faced with the challenge of designing the most cost-effective strategy in fighting drug abuse.

Alcohol abuse on the other hand is not considered a major health or social problem in Singapore because the rate of alcohol consumption is lower than that in Western countries (Ong and Isralowitz, 1996). Back, Jackson, Osman and Brady (2001) found marked difference in the consumption of alcohol between Singapore and American women with the latter consuming eight (8) times more alcoholic drinks on average per week compared to the former.

This paper will focus on current alcohol and drug rehabilitation strategies and discuss the challenges facing social workers and policy makers in Singapore. Data from a study conducted earlier will be presented in discussing some of these challenges, with specific focus on the problem of drug addiction.

DRUG AND ALCOHOL ABUSE IN SINGAPORE

The abuse of drugs in Singapore has seen periods of "highs and lows" over the last two decades. One of the indicators of the success of any drug prevention program is the number of first time addicts arrested. The National Council Against Drug Abuse (1998) noted that "if the number of new addicts is not reduced, the drug problem can never be effectively checked" (p. 49). Based on this indicator, the statistics since the mid-1990s shows promise for Singapore. Overall, since 1994, the number of drug addicts who have been arrested has dropped by almost one half (see Table 1).

The drug addiction problem has plagued the Malay community more than the other ethnic communities in Singapore. While the Malays make up only 14 percent of the total Singapore. population, they make up more than half of the drug addict population in the country. This over-representation has been studied by researchers in Singapore (e.g., Ong, 1989; Heng, 1995). The data presented in this paper also studied the Malay drug addicts in Singapore.

The alcohol abuse situation in Singapore is more difficult to ascertain. Unlike drug addiction, there is no compulsory treatment for alcoholics. A National Health Survey on a sample of 4,723 respondents conducted by the Ministry of Health in 1998 showed that while 40 percent consumed alcohol, less than 3 percent were regular drinkers (more than 4 days a week). Another 6 percent reported drinking frequently (1-3 days a week). There was no significant change from the data obtained in an earlier survey conducted in 1992. There were significantly more male than female drinkers in Singapore (5:1) (Ministry of Health, 1998). Kua (1995) also reported that more men than women were admitted to hospitals for alcohol related problems.

The 1998 government survey also reported that a crude prevalence of binge drinking was 5.1 percent in 1998 compared to 5.4 percent in 1992. Among the various ethnic groups in Singapore, the Indians (6.9%) had the highest prevalence of binge drinking, followed by the Chinese (5.5%) and Malays (1.8%) (Ministry of Health, 1998).

The Department of Customs and Excise in Singapore however, reported a slight increase in the level of alcohol consumption between 1993 and 1994. The revenue collected by the department increased by

TABLE 1. First-Time Drug Addicts Arrested in Singapore

YEAR	FIRST TIME ADDICTS	REPEAT ADDICTS	TOTAL
1994	1341	4824	6165
1995	978	5038	6016
1996	1421	4323	5744
1997	1134	3614	4752
1998	769	3733	4502
1999	786	3040	3826
2000	672	2485	3157

Source: Central Narcotics Bureau, 2000.

about 7.5% between 1993 (S$280.5 million) and 1994 (S$301.8 million) (Department of Custom and Excise, 1994). There is also an increasing trend in terms of deciliters consumed from 5.7 million in 1981 to 6.7 million in 1990 (Kua, 1995) to 7.5 million in 1994 (Department of Custom and Excise, 1994). Seng (1998) noted that there is also an increase of incidences of drunken driving, increasing from 299 drunken drivers arrested in 1991 to 538 in 1994. To address the increasing need for alcohol treatment, the Alcohol Treatment Centre of Woodbridge Hospital was established in 1993 and has treated over 400 patients in 4 years (Seng, 1998).

THE STRATEGIES FOR DRUG AND ALCOHOL CONTROL AND REHABILITATION

Singapore adopts an iron-fist approach towards drug control and rehabilitation in order to ensure that both demand for and supply of drugs are under control. In 1993 a high level government committee "Committee to Improve the Drug Situation in Singapore," was formed in order to formulate the new master plan to deal with the drug addiction problem. The recommendations of this committee form the cornerstone of Singapore's present anti-drug policies (National Council Against Drug Abuse, 1998).

Under this system, Singapore addresses the drug problem under four main coordinated and integrated strategies:

- Preventive Drug Education (PDE) which aims to prevent addiction;
- Enforcement, which aims to apprehend traffickers and addicts;

- Treatment and Rehabilitation, which aims to reform and deter addicts; and
- Aftercare and Continued Rehabilitation, which aims to reintegrate addicts into society.

Singapore has instituted the death penalty for anyone trafficking beyond a certain amount of a specific type of dangerous drug. Also, it is one of two the only two countries in the Asian region that have mandatory treatment policy for drug abusers (Scorzelli, 1987). Legislative amendments have been used in response to any deteriorating drug situation at a particular time. For example, the death penalty instituted in the Misuse of Drugs Act (Amendment) of 1975 was in response to the heroin epidemic that surged during that time. Similarly, the Intoxicating Substance Act, 1987 was instituted in response to the growing problem of inhalant abuse among Singaporean youths. The most recent amendment to the Misuse of Drugs Act (Amendment) 1998 was in response to the increasing dangerous use of Ice (methamphetamines) and the resulting high relapse rates. Table 2 summarizes the different legislative changes with regard to drug control and treatment over the past 40 years in Singapore.

The execution of both the drug control and rehabilitation strategies is done with the cooperation of both governmental and non-governmental agencies. Government agencies like the Central Narcotics Bureau (CNB) Prison's Department (Ministry of Home Affairs) collaborate with non-governmental agencies, such as the Singapore Anti-Narcotics Association (SANA), and Singapore Cooperative of Rehabilitative Enterprises (SCORE) to provide control, preventive, rehabilitative, and aftercare services in substance abuse.

THE TREATMENT OF DRUG ADDICTS IN SINGAPORE

Five Stage Rehabilitation at Drug Rehabilitation Centers

Rehabilitation and treatment programs of drug addicts in Singapore are targeted at the addicts who are identified on the basis of urine tests or medical examination. Having been confirmed as being drug addicts, they are committed by the Director of the Central Narcotics Bureau (CNB) for treatment and rehabilitation at one of the country's seven Drug Rehabilitation Centres (DRCs) for a period of 6 to 36 months. First time addicts go through a minimum mandatory 6-month stay. Re-

TABLE 2. Summary of Main Drug Legislation in Singapore

PERIOD	MAIN DRUG LEGISLATION IN SINGAPORE
1950s	**Dangerous Drug Ordinance, 1951** –opium, cannabis, morphine, cocaine, and heroin were specified as dangerous drugs and unauthorised possession is an offense often requiring mandatory treatment and rehabilitation of drug addicts
1970s	**Misuse of Drugs Act, 1973** –clear distinction between drug traffickers and drug abusers, which determine the level and kind of penalties and treatment to be given to offenders –127 substances were listed as controlled drugs in 3 classes –punishment for drug traffickers including caning and longer punishment was spelled out –Director of CNB empowered to obtain urine samples from suspected persons; to commit drug abusers to compulsory rehabilitation; and to impose period of compulsory supervision **Misuse of Drugs Act (Amendment), 1975** –death penalty was mandatory for traffickers of 15 grams of heroin or 30 grams of morphine –repeat offenders who commit the offense while under supervision would be sentenced to mandatory minimum term of 2 years imprisonment
1980s	**Intoxicating Substance Act, 1987** –inhalant abuse declared as an offense –suspected inhalant abusers are required to undergo a blood test –compulsory supervision (6 to 12 months) for inhalant abusers –fine for breaching supervision regulations –recalcitrant abusers may be admitted for compulsory treatment –offense to sell or supply or offer to sell or supply an intoxicating substance to any other person if he knows or has reasonable cause to believe that the intoxicating substance is, or its fumes, are likely to be used by the person receiving the intoxicating substance **Misuse of Drugs Act (Amendment), 1989** –definition of drug trafficker extended to include any person possessing 10 grams of cannabis resin or 3 grams of cocaine –drug penalty included any person in unauthorized possession of more than 1.2 kilograms of opium, more than 30 grams of cocaine, more than 500 grams of cannabis, or more than 200 grams of cannabis resin –mandatory minimum 2-year term of imprisonment was increased to "not more than 3 years for repeaters" –imposition of corporal punishment for severe indiscipline in the DRCs
1990s	**Misuse of Drugs Act (Amendment) 1998** –death penalty for anyone convicted of trafficking, importing, or exporting more than 250g of Ice –those caught with more than 25g of Ice or more than 10g of Ecstasy will automatically face charges of drug trafficking –mandatory jail terms of up to 13 years and 12 strokes of the cane for hardcore addicts

Sources: Ong, 1989; Ong & Isralowitz, 1996.

lapsed addicts often go through a minimum of a 12-month detention. In the DRC, they undergo a 5-stage program consisting of (1) detoxification; (2) recuperation and orientation; (3) physical training; (4) psychological counselling, and (5) work programs and education.

The "cold turkey" detoxification is medically supervised and lasts one week. According to Ong and Isralowitz (1996), this un-medicated withdrawal is intended to instil the knowledge that the addict can live without drugs and to discourage relapse. No visitors are allowed at this stage. Following a week of detoxification, the inmates spend the next week recuperating from the effects of detoxification and are assisted by the staff to understand the objectives of subsequent treatment. Ong and Isralowitz (1996) explain that indoctrination takes place during the third week. Here "the inmates are made aware of the legal aspects of drug control and punishment, the ill effects of drugs on health and mental well-being, the harmful effects of drug-taking on them, their families, communities, and country, as well as the realities of life and social obligations of each citizen" (p. 192). The two next phases of treatment are physical training and psychological counselling. This often takes place from the 4th to the 12th week. The inmates are required to take part in calisthenics physical fitness training to restore their physical health as well as to inculcate self-discipline (Ong and Isralowitz, 1996). Psychological counselling is provided by trained counsellors employed by the Prison's Department. The last phase in the DRC is the work program and education. It begins during the fourth month and continues until the inmate's release. "The main purpose here is to develop positive work habits and, where possible, to prepare the detoxicated addicts for employment upon release" (Ong and Isralowitz, 1996; p. 193).

Following this 5-stage program, the inmates are classified according to their rehabilitative needs and the extent to which they pose a threat to the security of the rehabilitation centres. Based on this assessment and classification the inmates are channelled into different programs, which come under the banner of the Community-Based Rehabilitation Program (CBR). Prior to the release to the CBR programs, the addicts are enrolled into a *Pre-Release Camp Program*. This is a month-long program that aims at inculcating in the addicts the necessary coping skills to deal with problems of readjusting to society. The addicts also learn to say "no" to the lure of drugs. Family members are also involved in the program to ensure that the addicts are able to adapt smoothly into society.

Community-Based Rehabilitation Program

Following the pre-release camp, the addicts are then assigned one of four CBR programs:

1. Residential Day-Release Scheme (Naltrexone);
2. Residential Day-Release Scheme (Non-Naltrexone);
3. Halfway-house (Naltrexone); and
4. Halfway-house (Non-Naltrexone).

One basis of assigning the addicts to the different programs is the level of family support. Addicts who are assessed as having good family support are more likely to be channelled to the residential day release schemes, while those assessed to have weaker family support are channelled to halfway houses. Naltrexone is a drug used as an antagonist to narcotics. It functions as a neuroblock that prevents the heroin consumer from feeling the euphoria associated with heroin consumption. Naltrexone tablets are administered to the inmates three times a week.

In the Day-Release Scheme the recovering addicts go to work during the day and return home to their families in the evenings. They have to observe curfew hours, generally from 7 P.M. to 7 A.M., and are tagged with an electronic monitor to ensure that they comply with the curfew hours.

The program for those in Halfway Houses is similar except that they return to the halfway houses in the evenings instead of their own homes. These halfway houses are managed by voluntary welfare organizations. At present there are 11 halfway houses in operation in Singapore. Within the halfway houses, three broad models exist–the religious model, the economic model and the therapeutic community (TC) model (Barrett & Lee, 2000).

The *religious model* sees Christianity, Islam and Buddhism as major religions used as the backbone to rehabilitation. Rehabilitation centers around worshiping and religious education. Very little professional counselling is found in such halfway houses (Barrett & Lee, 2000). The *economic model* uses work as the primary basis for rehabilitation. Residents of these halfway houses spend long hours working, often in manual jobs. Professional counselling and social work intervention is also limited in this model. Two of the 11 halfway houses have adopted the *therapeutic community* (TC) model of intervention. The focus is on using recovering addicts as change agents and positive role models. There is a more therapeutic approach in the TC rehabilitation model than in the other programs.

Compulsory Follow-Up

Once an addict is released from any of the Community Rehabilitation Centers, he is placed under a compulsory 2-year supervision program. In this program, the recovering addicts receive counselling from volunteer counsellors known as Volunteer Aftercare Officers. These volunteers undergo a series of training courses to equip them with basic listening and counselling skills. During the period of supervision, the supervisees are required to report regularly for routine urine tests at a designated police station. The frequency of the reporting can be on a 2-day, weekly or fortnightly cycle adjusted according to the progress made by the supervisee. CNB also conducts surprise tests on the supervisees from time to time (Ministry of Home Affairs, 1994: p. 23).

Enhanced Institutional Rehabilitation Programme (EIR)

The final program is the Enhanced Institutional Rehabilitation program. It is designed for "hard-core" or "recalcitrant" addicts who have to undergo the rehabilitation in the DRCs for the full 24-month term before they are eligible for the Day-Release Scheme. The "recalcitrant" (those who have been admitted to DRC three times or more) addicts are often distinguished from the "amenables" (those who have been admitted to the DRC for the first or second time). The former are subjected to a strict penal-like regime (lockup, drill, and physical exercise). This distinction is emphasized by the Committee to Improve the Drug Situation in Singapore:

> . . . for those who are responsive to our rehabilitative efforts, we should adopt a more compassionate and helpful approach. However, for the recalcitrant, we must adopt a firm and tough attitude against them. The recalcitrant or hardcore addicts must never be allowed to develop a "crutch mentality" by relying on the government for drug treatment all the time . . . The committee recommends that they should be kept progressively longer in the DRC. The DRC regime for such addicts should also be toughened with penal features so as to strengthen its deterrent effect. For the fifth timers and above, the committee recommends that the option of prosecuting them in the courts and subjecting them to a minimum

period of imprisonment and caning should be considered. The committee is of the view that adopting such a tough stand against hardcore addicts will in turn send a strong deterrent signal to new addicts that if they do not try to kick their habit quickly, they will also end up suffering similar consequences. (Ministry of Home Affairs, 1994: p. 20-21)

In 1988, the authorities introduced the Exit Counseling Program (ECP) and the Intensive Counseling Program (ICP) to cater to those drug abusers who "genuinely want to be free of their drug habit." The ECP was designed for first time abusers and provides a two-week rehabilitation program. The Committee to Improve the Drug Situation in Singapore, however, noted that feedback from the officers and counsellors indicate that the 2-week treatment was too short for it to be effective (Ministry of Home Affairs, 1994).

New Developing Programs

Until recently, partners and other family members have not been involved in the treatment program of the addicts. Recently however, "Family Support Seminars" have been organized. These sessions focus on the definition of the family's roles in the rehabilitation process of the recovering addicts. They also identify potential role conflicts between the addicts and their family members. The impact of this program on reducing the chances of relapse is still not known.

THE TREATMENT OF ALCOHOLICS IN SINGAPORE

The treatment of alcoholics in Singapore adopts a medical model. Those who are dependent on alcohol are treated at the alcohol treatment centres in major hospitals. The Alcohol Treatment Centre at Woodbridge Hospital (a psychiatric hospital in Singapore) is one of the treatment centres. Prior to the establishment of the centre,

> . . . treatment for alcoholics was mixed. While those with medical complications were treated at the medical units of general hospitals, those with cognitive impairments and behavioral problems landed in the psychiatric units of the general hospitals or the psychiatric hospitals. The treatment was mainly symptomatic with some counseling/therapy. There was hardly any structured treat-

ment program and hardly any attempt at rehabilitation. At the most the patients were encouraged to attend Alcoholics Anonymous meetings. (Seng, 1998, pp. 12-13)

The Alcohol Treatment Centre introduced a structured 4-6 week abstinence-based, multi-disciplinary treatment program. The multi-disciplinary team is comprised of psychiatrists, medical officers, social workers, psychologists, occupational therapists and nurses (Seng, 1998). The first stage of this inpatient treatment program is detoxification, which also addresses any medical complications that the alcoholic may have. This is followed by a structured daily psychoeducational program that includes attending educational lectures and group therapy. The alcoholics attend AA meetings in the evenings. Each patient also receives individual and family counseling provided by medical social workers. Follow up outpatient treatment, which includes medical consultation with a doctor and counseling sessions by medical social workers is also provided for each patient.

EMERGING CHALLENGES FOR DRUG AND ALCOHOL CONTROL AND TREATMENT

In 1998, the Singapore authorities crystallized a four-part strategy in battling the problem of drug addiction. These are: preventive education, enforcement, treatment and rehabilitation, and aftercare and continued rehabilitation. Using literature and data from a study conducted earlier, some emerging issues will be discussed in the context of this four-part strategy.

Preventive Drug Education

Implications of gateway drugs. Preventive drug education in Singapore has focused on the youth population in schools. This education has been targeted at youths-at-risk because the profile of many drug addicts showed certain common characteristics during their teens. Some of these characteristics include: poor school performance, being beyond parental control, and coming from low-income families (National Council Against Drug Abuse, 1998). While the efforts are commendable and in the right direction, Singapore is faced with the challenge of how to incorporate information on "gateway drugs" into these preventive drug education programs.

Studies have shown that many drug addicts start their drug use very early in their teens. Researchers like Chirstie et al. (1988), and Lopes, Lewis and Mann (1996) have found that alcohol often acts as a precursor to later drug use and to relapse. In Malaysia (a neighboring country to Singapore), Navaratnam and Foong (1989; 1990) found that heroin addiction was largely preceded by the use of nicotine (cigarette smoking), alcohol, and cannabis, while "other adjunctive drugs become important only after establishment of heroin addiction" (Navaratnam & Foong, 1989: p. 608). A 1998 study by Osman also found that alcohol and cannabis use often preceded the use of heroin among Malay drug addicts. Many of the respondents in this study indicated that they began to use heroin after alcohol and cannabis failed to give them the same level of euphoria ("high") that they were used to.

The presence of these gateway drugs suggests the need to address their use among the young. Researchers have shown that drug addicts begin smoking and drinking as early as age 10 (e.g., Navaratnam & Koong, 1989). The current strategy of preventive drug education emphasized the ill effects of drugs like heroin and morphine. Including the dangers of nicotine and alcohol in the drug prevention program will highlight that these gateway drugs are equally dangerous and should be avoided. Moreover, while there has been legislation to curb the use of alcohol and nicotine among minors, youngsters' access to places where such substances are readily available (e.g., night clubs and pubs) also needs to be addressed.

Implications of parental substance abuse. Cigarette smoking and alcohol consumption are common among parents of drug abusers. Osman (1998) found that when comparing individuals who were considered to be successful in their rehabilitation to those who relapsed, the latter were more likely to have parents who were consuming alcohol regularly. The challenge for preventive drug education is the involvement of family members who are themselves consuming alcohol. Families need to be educated on the potential effects of their alcohol use on the children's heroin addiction. Modelling of smoking and drinking behaviour in the homes of these at-risk youths will increase the likelihood of their involvement in these gateway drugs, and subsequent involvement in other drugs like heroin. Often these parents themselves do not see the dangers of these gateway drugs. The challenge of preventive drug education is thus to "convert" these parents into allies in the fight against drug abuse.

Equipping families with knowledge and skills. Preventive education should also include equipping families with the skills and knowledge to guide their young offspring. Oftentimes these families are not equipped to respond to their children's queries regarding the rationale for certain rules and prohibitions of behaviors, such as not smoking or not drinking. The traditional top-down approach or "parents know best" approach (a common parenting style among Singapore parents) is less effective in this day and age where youths are exposed to many different media. They are curious and they need rational answers. Parents must be prepared for such situations.

Enforcement

In Singapore, stringent anti-drug laws have been instituted and their enforcement has been going on for several decades. The government has prosecuted 287 drug traffickers in the last 10 years (National Council Against Drug Abuse, 1998). Yet the drug menace still exists. The availability of substitute drugs has emerged as a challenge for the enforcement arm of the drug control and rehabilitation program.

The history of drug abuse in Singapore shows the movement of different types of drugs into the forefront. In the early 1970s, after the opium problem was somewhat resolved, cannabis and heroin came into the picture. When legislation against heroin abuse was toughened, by the 1980s, inhalants started to dominate the drug scene. Then came designer drugs like Ice (metha-amphetamine hydrochloride) and Ecstasy (methylenediocy-methamphetamine). The pattern shows that in four decades, the drug scene has always included new substitute drugs. The challenge is to collaborate closely with neighboring countries to anticipate the intrusion of new substances and to prevent their spread as early as possible.

Treatment and rehabilitation. One of the strategies of understanding what works in treatment and rehabilitation is to compare relapsed cases with successful cases. Differences between both groups may suggest important indicators of success. The findings of a study conducted by the author (Osman, 1998) are used to discuss the challenges facing treatment and rehabilitation and aftercare services for drug addicts.

This study compared two groups of addicts, those who relapsed and success cases. Success was measured by non-consumption of drugs within two years following the release from a drug treatment program. To control for confounding variables, the study's sample was limited to a cohort of first time drug addicts. Among the variables studied were demographic, familial, individual, and religious. The study was also confined to Malay addicts, who were over-represented among the drug addict population in Singapore. Bivariate analysis found significant differences in several factors. Success cases were more likely to have higher levels of education, more likely to be married and less likely to have a history of criminal involvement (see Table 3).

In terms of familial variables, the study found significant difference between familial substance abuse history and family cohesion (Cronbach alpha = .72) between the two groups (Table 3 and Table 4). Relapsed cases were more likely to have family members who were consuming alcohol and/or abusing heroin, and less likely to perceive their families as cohesive compared to the success cases.

Five individual variables were found to differ significantly between the two groups. The success cases were more likely to engage in regular employment compared to the relapsed cases (see Table 3). They were also more likely to have higher levels of self satisfaction, motivation, hope, and more positive personal values (see Table 4). The Cronbach alpha for these latter scales were .70, .47, .70 and .54 respectively.

Four of the five religious variables studied were found to differ significantly between the two groups of addicts. Success cases were more likely to have higher levels of intrinsic religious commitment, more personal religious experiences, practiced their religion more regularly, and have higher levels of religious education and knowledge compared to the relapsed cases. The Cronbach alpha for these religious scales were .70, .71, .64 and .59 respectively.

The findings of this study suggests that there are risk factors to relapse as well as factors that lead to success in kicking drug addiction. The study also found that the average time lapse between release from DRC and onset of relapse was about 4 months.

The current treatment and rehabilitation programs do not distinguish between those who are at risk of relapse and those who are not. The limited resources that are available could best be allocated efficiently with the identification of those ex-addicts who are at risk of relapse. The challenge for treatment and rehabilitation is to design programs that meet the needs of both those at risk of relapse and those who have higher potential to succeed after treatment. The first four months are crucial for those at risk of relapse, and therefore require the need for close supervision.

Familial Intervention. The important role of the family in drug rehabilitation has been underscored by many researchers (e.g., Daley, 1989; Gibson, Sorensen, Wermuth & Brenal, 1992; Karim, 1992; Kapoor, 1992; Liddle and Dakof, 1995). The author's findings that the relapsed cases are more likely to have a family member who is a substance

TABLE 3. Variables Affecting Treatment Outcome of Addicts

| | Treatment Outcome | | | |
	Success (n)	Relapsed (n)	χ^2	df
Educational Level			13.3*	6
Primary school and below	13	20		
Secondary (not complete)	9	10		
VITB/ITE (technical education)	8	3		
GCE 'N' Level	-	3		
GCE 'O'/ 'A' Level	6	2		
Marital Status			9.3**	2
Married	13	3		
Single	19	31		
Divorced	4	6		
Family member(s) regularly drink alcohol			27.9****	1
Yes	2	27		
No	26	10		
Family member(s) taking drugs			5.28*	1
Yes	13	25		
No	23	15		
History of criminal involvement			4.23*	1
Yes	14	25		
No	22	15		
Nature of employment			11.98***	1
Regular employment	20	7		
Irregular employment	16	33		

*p < .05, ** p < .01, *** p < .001, **** p < .0001

abuser suggests the existence of two distinct groups of families: the "addicted families" and "families of addicts." The former are families who have more than one member who are addicted to substances like alcohol and/or drugs. These family members might be modeling the behavior. Moreover, family members' involvement in drugs results in close proximity and availability of drugs to recovering drug users leaving treatment. Some of the respondents admitted that their first intake of drug following release from DRC was with a family member. The presence

TABLE 4. T-Tests of Familial, Individual, and Religious Variables and Treatment Outcome

| | Treatment Outcome | | | | |
| | Success | | Relapsed | | |
Scales	Mean	sd	Mean	sd	T
Familial Scales					
Family Relationship	44.19	7.95	41.98	6.12	1.353
Family Cohesion	21.81	3.72	20.23	3.16	1.984*
Family Communication	17.86	2.75	17.63	2.45	0.394
Individual Scales					
Self Satisfaction	18.44	3.33	14.28	3.19	5.559****
Personal Values	19.83	1.98	18.83	2.35	2.029*
Motivation	17.50	2.38	15.75	2.64	3.037**
Hope	24.97	2.96	23.68	2.32	2.636**
Religious Scales					
Intrinsic Religious Commitment	15.42	2.02	12.40	2.51	5.798****
Extrinsic Religious Commitment	11.64	1.88	11.28	2.09	0.799
Personal Religious Experiences	20.44	2.83	16.68	3.68	5.034****
Religious Practices	19.11	4.07	17.27	3.58	2.078*
Religious Education/Knowledge	16.50	2.65	15.15	2.47	2.294*

*p < .05, **p < .01, ***p < .001, ****p < .0001

of a family member involved in alcohol and drug consumption creates a family environment and culture that sends a message to these addicts that these activities are accepted and tolerated. Thus, addicts released from DRC who have a family member who is also an addict or alcohol abuser may be at greater risk than their counterparts who do not have a substance abusing family member.

The concept of "addicted families" is different from the concept of "families of addicts." "Addicted families" are characterized by the existence of substance abuse problem faced by more than one member, often a parent and a child. They may have a different set of needs from families of addicts. "Families of addicts" are families who only have one member involved in substance abuse. This is similar to Goodwin's (1985) typology of "familial" and "non familial" alcoholism. The former, he argues, has a specific biological and genetic basis to alcoholism, while the latter is determined by environmental factors.

Family cohesion was found to be an important familial variable. Family cohesion refers to the extent to which family members feel close together and will do things together. Therefore, intervention with "families of addicts" or with "addicted families" must include the goal of enhancing family cohesion. This will in turn create and enhance the structure and organization in the lives of these addicts and their families.

Thus a related challenge is to accommodate the families in the treatment and rehabilitation process. At this time, families are not part of the rehabilitation programs that addicts undergo. The drug rehabilitation centres where these programs are implemented are high security institutions that have restrictions on admission of civilians. Since the treatment programs for addicts are currently compulsory, the feasibility of including families in the treatment program needs to be assessed immediately.

Indigenous model of practice. Another challenge facing treatment and rehabilitation services in Singapore is the documentation of what works. Treatment models have traditionally been adopted from the West. Service providers in Singapore need to begin evaluating their own work and documenting if these treatment modalities are relevant to the context of Singapore. The challenge is to develop an effective indigenous model of practice with drug abusers in this country.

Aftercare and Rehabilitation

Aftercare and rehabilitation are crucial in combating the drug problem. As indicated, Singapore has instituted compulsory supervision periods for ex-addicts released from DRCs. Nonetheless, there are several challenges facing the aftercare and rehabilitation services.

Closer supervision for high risk group. The first few months following release from DRC is the most crucial period for recovery. The current after care supervision is done by Central Narcotics Bureau's officers whose focus is on the drug taking itself. These officers monitor the addicts through the regular urine screening. The psychosocial aspects of after care are often left to the Volunteer Aftercare Officers. The high risk group requires more intensive supervision and assistance in aftercare and the volunteer officers may not be equipped to meet the expectations of such intensive treatment. Full time trained counselors and social workers should be tasked to provide closer aftercare service for the high risk group.

Employment opportunities. Addicts released from DRC need to be helped in obtaining and maintaining regular employment. While many might have had a history of irregular employment and may still prefer such form of employment, efforts must be invested in helping addicts get regular employment. Studies have found that employment has a significant impact on self esteem, motivation, and sense of hope (DeJong and Henrich, 1980; Joe, Simpson and Sells, 1994; Osman, 1998). In the study by the author highlighted above, many relapsed cases were found to choose irregular employment because they were not sure if they could meet the demands of regular employment. Due to their general low educational qualifications, many felt that they did not have the chance to obtain or maintain regular employment (Osman 1998). Any employment given to ex-addicts should be within an environment that includes non-addicts. This will enhance the ex-addicts' feeling that they are accepted and can function in society. Close supervision and intervention focused on problem solving skills are needed for "high risk" groups in such employment settings.

The task of educating potential employers on the employability of ex-addicts is not an easy one. The issue of employment opportunities is even more crucial today given the economic crisis that is faced by the Asian region. The preference for irregular employment by drug addicts also relates to their inability to delay gratification, which might be lower among the relapsed addicts. Irregular employment allows a salary to be obtained on a daily basis and not subject to deductions for compulsory savings. Many addicts do not realize the long term benefits of delaying their gratification of receiving daily earnings. In Singapore, the compulsory Central Provident Fund (CPF) contributions should be viewed as an investment for the future. In addition, since part of the savings account can be used for hospitalization expenses, it is also a form of insurance. Regular employment also provides benefits such as medical and annual leave. It also provides regularity and stability in the lives of ex-addicts. Thus, the challenge for aftercare services is to enhance a positive attitude towards delayed gratification in relation to employment.

The importance of religious guidance. The importance of religious variables in rehabilitation is worth discussing since intrinsic religious commitment was found to differentiate between relapsed and success cases. Most respondents in the Osman (1998) study found the religious guidance and counseling that they received in DRCs useful. However, many were not able to maintain the practice and internalize the teachings once they left the DRC. To have high intrinsic religious commitment, one needs to be able to internalize the values and teachings of religion and understand it in relation to one's behavior.

For many, religious experience in DRC was like an awakening. However, many "dosed off" after their release. A follow up program is needed for addicts who have been released to continue receiving religious guidance. This will enhance their ability to internalize the religious teachings and reduce the chances of returning to drinking alcohol and consuming drugs.

Other Challenges

More research on drug addiction. Drug addiction is a multi-dimensional phenomenon that can only be understood with continuous research. There is still a large scope of research areas that need to be explored in Singapore. For example, an area of research that needs future action is the phenomenon of the "addicted families." Do they actually exist? What is the prevalence rate? Who are they and what are the dynamics in such families? Do they have different needs from families of other drug addicts (in which no other family members are addicts) or families free from drug addiction?

The findings of the study presented above suggests that the importance of understanding the biological explanation of addiction. Future research may focus on children of drug addicts who are raised in different environments from their parents, as has been done in studies of children of alcoholics. A longitudinal study involving these children may shed further light on the biological perspective of addictions in Singapore.

The prevalence of alcohol consumption among youths is yet another area that needs to be researched. As a gateway drug, the prevalence of alcohol consumption and abuse indicates the potential for future drug abuse.

Community's response. The social environment that ex-addicts operate in is crucial, since a misfit between an individual and his social environment may result in his return to drug use. The community has an important role to play in their acceptance or rejection of the ex-addict who returns to live among it. The challenge for the field and for the social work profession is to involve the community in the rehabilitation process of addicted individuals.

CONCLUSION

This paper has reviewed the strategies of drug and alcohol control and rehabilitation in Singapore. Singapore has adopted a hard-line stand in the fight against drug abuse. The death penalty is meted out for those trafficking a large amount of drugs. Treatment and rehabilitation is compulsory for those addicts who are arrested. The alcohol abuse situation however, is not alarming. Several challenges with regards to drug control and rehabilitation have been discussed in the paper. It was shown that there are several new areas that need to be addressed by the authorities involved in fighting the drug problem.

The problem of drug addiction is not new. However, the approaches to dealing with it must constantly be evaluated and reviewed. More research needs to be conducted to provide future directions in terms of prevention, treatment, aftercare and rehabilitation. Innovative modalities need to be invented to keep pace with changing times. This is even more crucial given the limited resources available, especially with the gloomy economic forecast for the region. While the role of social workers has been limited, their involvement in the prevention and rehabilitation of drug addicts in Singapore, and particularly with their families and community, can play a crucial role in the future.

REFERENCES

Back, S. E., Jackson, J., Osman, M. M., & Brady, K.T. (2001). Substance use and trauma across cultures. Paper presented at the Annual Meeting of the Southeastern Psychological Association, Atlanta, GA.

Barrett, M.E., & Lee, A. (2000). *Report on Evaluation of Halfway Houses in Singapore.* Unpublished report. Singapore: SCORE.

Central Narcotics Bureau, 2000. Annual Report. Singapore: Central Narcotics Bureau.

Christie, K.A., Burke, J.D.J., Regier, D.A., Rae, D.S., Boyd, J.H. & Locke, B.Z. (1988). Epidemiologic evidence for early onset of mental disorders and higher risk of drug abuse in young adults. *American Journal of Psychiatry, 145,* 971-975.

Daley, D.C. (1989). Five perspectives on relapse and dependency. *Journal of Chemical Dependence and Treatment, 2,* 3-26.

DeJong, R. & Henrich, G. (1980). Follow up results of a behavior modification program for juvenile drug addicts. *Addictive Behaviors,* 5 (1), 49-57.

Department of Customs and Excise (1994). Annual Report. Singapore Department of Customs and Excise: Singapore.

Gibson, D.R., Sorensen, J.L., Wermuth, L., & Bernal, G. (1992). Families are helped by drug treatment. *The International Journal of the Addictions, 27,* 961-978.

Goodwin, D.W. (1985). Alcoholism and genetics. *Archives of General Psychiatry, 28,* 238-243.

Heng, F.H.M. (1995). *Ethnicity and drug abuse: The case of the Singapore Malays.* Unpublished doctoral dissertation. The University of Hull.

Joe, G.W., Simpson, D.D., & Sells, S.B. (1994). Treatment process and relapse to opioid use during methadone maintenance. *American Journal of Drug and Alcohol Abuse,* 20(2).

Kapoor, S.K. (1992). Role of the family in prevention and control of substance abuse: Different strategies in prevention. Paper presented at the 14th IFNGO Conference, Malaysia.

Kua, E.H. (1995). *One too many: Overcoming Alcoholism.* Armour Publishing: Singapore.

Liddle, H.A., & Dakof, G.A. (1995). Efficacy of family therapy for drug abuse: Promising but not definitive. *Journal of Marital and Family Therapy, 21,* 511-543.

Lopes, C.S., Lewis, G. & Mann, A. (1996). Psychiatric and alcohol disorders as risk factors for drug abuse: A case control study among adults in Rio de Janeiro, Brazil. *Social Psychiatry and Psychiatric Epidemiology, 31,* 355-363.

Ministry of Health (1998). National Health Survey 1998: Singapore. Ministry of Health.

Ministry of Home Affairs (1994). *The Report of the Committee to Improve the Drug Situation in Singapore.* Singapore. Ministry of Home Affairs.

National Council Against Drug Abuse (1998). *Towards A Drug-Free Singapore: Strategies, Policies and Programmes Against Drugs.* Singapore: NCADA.

Navaratnam, V. & Foong, K. (1990). Adjunctive drug use among opiate addicts. *Current Medical Research and Opinion, 11,* 611-619.

Navaratnam, V. & Foong, K. (1989). Sequence of onset of different drug use among opiate addicts. *Current Medical Research and Opinion, 11,* 600-609.

Ong, T.H. (1989). *Drug Abuse in Singapore: A psychological perspective.* Singapore: Hillview Publications.

Ong, T.H. & Isralowitz, R. (1996). *Substance Abuse in Singapore: Illegal drugs, inhalants, and alcohol.* Singapore: Toppan Company.

Osman, M.M. (1998). *Predicting rehabilitated or relapsed status of Malay drug addicts in Singapore: The role of familial, individual, religious, and social support factors.* Unpublished doctoral dissertation, University of Illinois at Urbana-Champaign, Illinois.

Scorzelli, J. (1987). *Drug Abuse: Preventions and rehabilitations in Malaysia.* Malaysia: University Kebangsaan Malaysia. They spend $35 million on drugs a year. (1998, February 1). *The Straits Times.*

Seng, B.K. (1998). Predicting treatment outcomes in alcoholics. *Unpublished Master of Social Science Thesis. Department of Social Work and Psychology, National University of Singapore. Singapore.*

A Preliminary Exploration
of Immigrant Substance Abusers
from the Former Soviet Union Living
in Israel, Germany and the United States:
A Multi-National Perspective

Richard Isralowitz
Shulamith Lala Ashenberg Straussner
Irmgard Vogt
Victor Chtenguelov

SUMMARY. The Former Soviet Union (FSU) has historically been seen as having an unusually large population of individuals with alcohol problems. Since the fall of the communist regime, a growing drug abusing population has become visible. With the large migration of its residents to western countries and to Israel, the rates of alcohol and drug

Richard Isralowitz, PhD, is Professor, School of Social Work and Director, Regional Alcohol and Drug Abuse Resources Center, Ben Gurion University, Israel. Shulamith Lala Ashenberg Straussner, DSW, CAS, is Professor, Ehrenkranz School of Social Work, New York University, New York, USA. She is the Editor of *JSWPA*. Irmgard Vogt, PhD, is Professor, University of Applied Sciences, Department of Social Work and Health, Frankfurt am Main, Germany. Victor Chtenguelov, MD, is Deputy Director of Substance Abuse, Ukrainian Research Institute on Social and Forensic Psychiatry and Substance Abuse, Kiev, Ukraine.

Special thanks to Drs. Helen Kagan, Norma Phillips and RoseMarie Perez Foster.

[Haworth co-indexing entry note]: "A Preliminary Exploration of Immigrant Substance Abusers from the Former Soviet Union Living in Israel, Germany and the United States: A Multi-National Perspective." Isralowitz et al. Co-published simultaneously in *Journal of Social Work Practice in the Addictions* (The Haworth Social Work Practice Press, an imprint of The Haworth Press, Inc.) Vol. 2, No. 3/4, 2002, pp. 119-136; and: *International Aspects of Social Work Practice in the Addictions* (ed: Shulamith Lala Ashenberg Straussner, and Larry Harrison) The Haworth Social Work Practice Press, an imprint of The Haworth Press, Inc., 2002, pp. 119-136. Single or multiple copies of this article are available for a fee from The Haworth Document Delivery Service [1-800-HAWORTH, 9:00 a.m. - 5:00 p.m. (EST). E-mail address: getinfo@haworthpressinc.com].

problems among these immigrants appear to be disproportionally high, although reliable data are lacking. The purpose of this article is to summarize exploratory data regarding alcohol and other drug use among immigrants from the Former Soviet Union living in Israel, Germany and the United States, and to identify further research needs and implications for treatment and policy. *[Article copies available for a fee from The Haworth Document Delivery Service: 1-800-HAWORTH. E-mail address: <getinfo@haworthpressinc.com> Website: <http://www.HaworthPress.com> © 2002 by The Haworth Press, Inc. All rights reserved.]*

KEYWORDS. Drug and alcohol abuse, Russian immigrants, heroin addicts in Former Soviet Union, Israel, Germany, United States

INTRODUCTION

Throughout history, the use and abuse of alcohol and other drugs (AOD) have been grounded in social contexts that tend to vary over time and location (Orlandi, 1995). The drug type and how it is used, the social strata of those who use it, the kinds of situations in which it is used, the treatment approach, as well as the political, legal and social reactions to its use are all reflective of a particular ethnic and socio-cultural context (Goode, 1989, Orlandi, 1995; Straussner, 2001a; b). "An individual's cultural affiliation often determines the person's values and attitudes about health issues, responses to messages, and even the use of alcohol, tobacco and other drugs" (Wright, 1994:1). Although there is some literature regarding the relation between specific cultures and the use of specific substances (Isralowitz, 2002; Orlandi, 1995; Straussner, 2001a), less is known about the relationship between international migration and the use and abuse of alcohol and other drugs. Some researchers believe that the trauma of immigration and difficulties with the process of acculturation and assimilation are linked to the development of emotional and behavioral problems, including substance abuse (Goodenow & Espin, 1993; James; 1997; Krupinski; 1984; Oetting & Beauvais, 1990; Ortega, Rosenbeck, Alegria, & Desai, 2000; Rogler, Cortes & Malgady, 1991, Westermeyer, 1993), others found, however, that immigrants are less likely to have substance use disorders than native born populations, even those from the same socioeconomic (Van Geest & Johnson, 1997) and ethnocultural backgrounds (Escobar, Hoyos, & Gara, 2000; Powles, Macaskill, Hopper & Ktenas,

1991). These contradictory findings point to the need for further exploration of the interrelationship between ethnicity, culture, migration and the use and abuse of AOD. Do immigrants with a substance abuse problem develop it after or before migration? Is there a gender difference among substance abusing immigrants compared to the local population? Do people from the same culture who migrate to different countries adapt their use of substances to the local norm, that is, how do substance use patterns of immigrants compare to people in their home country and to the local population? What are the implications for prevention and treatment of these immigrants? What are the policy implications?

This paper attempts to begin to explore these questions by providing preliminary data regarding the use of AOD by immigrants from the Former Soviet Union (FSU) who settled in Israel, Germany and the United States following the fall of the Soviet Union in the 1980s. In each of these countries, the immigrants from the FSU have been recognized as having an unusually high rate of substance abuse in comparison to other immigrants, and possibly even native populations (Hasin, Rahav, Meydan & Newmark, 1998; Kagan & Shafer, 2001; Vogt & Schmid 2000). Yet, research studies on this population are very limited despite some preliminary data that are beginning to accumulate in Israel and Germany. Before presenting what little is known about these immigrants, it is important to understand the scope of alcohol and drugs in the former Soviet Union, particularly Russia and Ukraine, the two FSU countries with the greatest number of emigrants to Israel and Western countries.

The Use and Abuse of Alcohol and Other Drugs in the Former Soviet Union

Although there is a lack of reliable data, it is believed that as much as 20-25% of the population in the FSU have alcohol and/or drug problems (Davis, 1994; Spector, 1997 a; b). In 1985, the rate of consumption of alcoholic beverages in the Soviet Union was estimated to be three times higher than that in the United States (Segal, 1990). More recently, it has been reported that out of 148 million people, there are approximately 1.5 million chronic alcoholics and three to four times more the number of heavy drinkers (Davis, 1994; Kagan & Shafer, 2001). The current life expectancy of Russian men is 59 years, less than that of men in three-fourths of the world's countries. The main cause of this early death is attributed to Russian life style, particularly heavy smoking and drinking. According to a news item reported in the *Washington Post* in August, 2001 ("Smoking Shortens Life Expectancy. . ." p. 1), "Nearly two-thirds of Russian men smoke, compared to one-fourth of U.S. men. In addition, the typical Russian male drinks a pint of pure alcohol every two days."

Alcohol is not the only substance abused in the FSU. More than two million drug addicts are estimated to be living there and much of the problem stems from cheap opium products, including heroin, coming from Pakistan, Afghanistan and other countries of Central Asia (Spector, 1997a). Marijuana, cocaine, heroin and prescription drugs are also being abused on a large scale (Kagan & Shafer, 2001). In addition, it is common for many adolescents to be involved with sniffing inhalants, such as glue, paint and homemade synthetic drugs (Davis, 1994; Spector, 1997b).

In Ukraine, the number of officially registered drug abusers is 90,000 in a population of 48 million, or almost 2 percent of the population. It is estimated, however, that the actual number is three to seven times higher (Chtenguelov, 2002), or between 6 and 14 percent. The main drug of choice is opium straw extract. Among young people there has been a growing use of marijuana and synthetic "dance" (or "club") drugs that are similar to ephedrine. These dance drugs are typically used in tablet form, while other stimulant-type substances are injected (Chtenguelov, 2002). One consequence of the growing drug use in Ukraine has been a dramatic increase of HIV infection. Among the 37,000 individuals who have diagnosed as being infected with HIV at the end of 2000, the main cause of the infection has been attributed to heroin that is sold in preloaded syringes, which are then reused by other addicts (Chtenguelov, 2002).

THE ROLES OF RELIGION AND ETHNIC FACTORS

Studies of various ethnocultural groups indicate that the quantity and the kind of substances used do vary among different groups (Straussner, 2001a, b). Therefore, it is important to examine the use of substances by different ethnic groups even if they come from the same country.

In line with communist ideology, the majority of the former Soviets grew up without any religious or spiritual beliefs (Kagan and Shaefer, 2001). Nonetheless, much of the emigration from the FSU has been related to ethnic and cultural/religious identification of individuals and families. Those whose families traced their original ethnocultural identification to being Jewish, or who were from ethnic German backgrounds, among others, had maintained or were forced to maintain these identities that were stamped in the internal passports carried by each individual. With the fall of the Soviet Union, both Jews and ethnic Germans were provided easier access and greater support to emigrate than were people from other ethnic or religious cultural groups. Soviets of Jewish background were openly welcomed as citizens in Israel, and those of German background were allowed to emigrate and given full citizen rights in Germany. While Soviet immigrants to the United States (and Canada) included both Jews and non-Jews, the vast majority appear to be Jewish (see Table 1).

The abuse of and dependence on alcohol among Jews appears to be lower than that of other populations in Eastern Europe and Western countries (Glassner & Berg, 1985; Keller, 1970; Monteiro, Klein, & Schuckit, 1991; Straussner, 2001c). While there is no data regarding drug use among Jews in FSU or European countries, Straussner (2001c) found that the use of illicit drugs among Jewish Americans appears to be similar to or even slightly higher than the general population in the U.S. These ethnocultural and religious dynamics need to be kept in mind when examining substance abuse and treatment implications among immigrants from the FSU.

SUBSTANCE ABUSE AMONG FSU IMMIGRANTS IN ISRAEL, GERMANY AND U.S.A.

The data regarding substance abuse among FSU immigrants who settled in Israel, Germany and the United States were collected independ-

TABLE 1. Immigrants from FSU Residing in Different Countries

Country	Number/Percentage	% of Total Population
Germany	1.5 million	2
Ethnic Germans	99%	
Jews	< 1%	
Israel	1 million	18
Jews*	66%	
Non-Jews*	33%	
United States	400,000	< .01
Jews*	70%	
Non-Jews*	30%	

* Official data not available. Estimates based on discussion with experts.

ently and are based on different methods utilized in each of these countries. These data are descriptive and preliminary, and mostly based on exploratory studies and clinical observations of the authors of this article. Thus it is difficult to compare the findings. Nonetheless, given the paucity of information regarding this population, it is anticipated that this information will provide the basis for more systematic data collection by in the future.

It is not unusual for immigrants to cope with stresses associated with immigration and adjustment to the new country by increasing their use of alcohol or turning to the use of drugs (Westermeyer, 1993). Moreover, it is believed that:

> the greater availability, lower cost, higher level of alcohol concentration, and higher quality of alcoholic beverages in the United States [and Germany] results in increased drinking among these [FSU] immigrants who were already reliant on the use of alcohol to cope with life. Additionally, due to years of poor diet and medical care, Russian-speaking immigrants often arrive with serious medical problems. Such problems may require prolonged use of prescribed medications leading to potential abuse and dependency on the prescribed drugs. . . . [Moreover] Due to the lack of education and prevention efforts in the [former Soviet Union] young people are not familiar with the dangerous consequences of illegal drugs and often find themselves [caught in the . . . drug culture scene] (Kagan and Shafer, 2001: 261).

Israel

The immigration of people from the FSU to Israel since 1989 was so overwhelming that government authorities could barely manage the detailed inspection of those who met acceptance criteria based on religious grounds, let alone examine the mental and physical health, criminal experience or addiction to illegal substances of the immigrants (Isralowitz, 2001). During the one-year period of 1990-1991, the number of FSU immigrants was approximately 370,000–a number nearly equal to those from the Soviet Union who had settled in Israel over the entire previous forty years of its existence as a modern state. By 2000, the population of FSU immigrants since 1989 reached 1,000,000 representing nearly 18% of the current residents in the country, although in the past year this number has decreased to about 850,000 as a result of relocation to other western countries, principally, the United States and Canada.

Prior to the massive immigration, about 95 percent of the illegal drug users in Israel were of Sephardic background (i.e., people of North African origin, primarily from Morocco and Tunisia), who prefer smoking the substance (Isralowitz, 2001; Straussner, 2001c). Studies indicated that these addicts tended to be male (about 80%), between the ages of 18 and 30, poorly educated (less than high school education), and of low socio-economic status (Isralowitz, 2001, Isralowitz, Abu Saad, & Telias, 1996; Isralowitz, Telias, & Abu Saad, 1994; Isralowitz, Telias, & Zighelbaum, 1992).

Soon after 1990, due to the wave of immigration from the FSU, the profile of the nation's heroin addict population changed. Presently, it is estimated that 25 percent of Israel's 25,000 drug addicts (Bar-Hamburger, 2001; Elisha, 1998) (out of a total population of around 6 million) came to the country after 1989 from Russia, Ukraine and other Soviet republics. The vast majority of these addicts (97%) reported immigrating to Israel already addicted, and of this group 14% reported that they were released by officials in order to immigrate to Israel (Isralowitz, 2002).

Recent research findings (Isralowitz, 2002; Isralowitz & Borkin, 2002) comparing the psychosocial profile and patterns of substance between 167 FSU and 154 Israeli male and female heroin addicts are reflected in Table 2.

Data regarding alcohol abusers in Israel is limited. It is estimated that there are between 50,000 and 100,000 alcoholics (0.8%-1.5% of the total population), the majority of them born outside of Israel, mainly in FSU and other Eastern European countries, or coming from Middle East/North Africa. Those from the FSU tend to be better educated men, around age 40, likely to be married and to be unemployed (see Peleg-Oren, Rahav & Teichman, this volume).

Germany

Since the late 1980s, when exit restrictions were eased in the Soviet Union, approximately 1.5 million Russian-speaking immigrants relocated to Germany, comprising about 2% of German's population of 82 million. According to German law, people with German "blood-bonds" referred to as "ethnic Germans," are entitled to a German passport, and therefore all the benefits of citizenship, upon arrival in Germany. However, after the "flood gates" were open to receive immigrants from the

TABLE 2. Comparison of Drug Abusers from FSU (N = 167; men = 114; women = 53) and Native Israelis (N = 154; men = 93; women = 61) in percentages

Variable	FSU	Israelis
Completed high school/trade school or other form of higher education	80	45
History of imprisonment	44	57
History of psychiatric hospitalization (mainly for detoxification)	19	18
Physically abused as a child	38	32
Sexually abused as a child	11	22
Men	5	15
Women	25	37
Alcohol abuse by parents		
Mothers	11	5
Fathers	34	31
Drug use by parents		
Mothers	4	2
Fathers	4	6
Alcohol abuse by parents of female addicts		
Mothers	14	5
Fathers	45	23
Drug use by parents of female addicts		
Mothers	8	4
Fathers	4	9
Alcohol/Drug use *while* in treatment	66	16
Believed able to stop drug use if wanted	72	49
Primary reason to stop drug use		
Health (men only)	34	57
Regain custody of children (women only)	74	43

former Soviet Union, serious social and health problems arose, along with political and social pressures to stem the tide of this immigration. Consequently, a language test was introduced for all ethnic Germans wanting to immigrate. No attempt was made, however, to restrict ethnic German immigration based on criminal record, mental health status, or the use and abuse of harmful substances (Eichenhofer, 1999). Research about immigrants from the former Soviet Union is limited; many are German speaking and thus tend to meld within the general population (Riecken, 1999; Strobl & Kuehnel, 2000), particularly since specific questions regarding country of birth among those with German citizenship tend not to be asked by researchers.

In addition to ethnic Germans, approximately 140,000 Jewish immigrants from the former Soviet Union came to Germany as refugees in the last 15 years (Bade & Oltmer, 1999, Federal Government's Commissioner for Foreigners' Issues, 2000). Unlike ethnic Germans, they do not hold a German passport, but do have an unlimited residence permit.

The reported prevalence rate of illicit drug users among German adults aged 18 to 59 for the year 2000 was approximately 5% of the population; the primary drug of choice during that year was cannabis (Kraus & Augustin, 2001). Results of preliminary studies in Germany of substance abusing ethnic immigrants from the FSU and other eastern European countries (Boos-Nuenning et al., 2002; Dill et al., 2002; Strobl & Kuehnel, 2000; Riecken, 1999; Schwichtenberg & Weig, 1999; Vogt & Schmid, 2000) are summarized in Table 3.

It is estimated that of all those in treatment for substance abuse problems, the proportion of immigrants from the FSU with alcohol problems is about 2% and the proportion of those with illicit drug problems is between 4 to 6 percent. FSU immigrants to Germany tend to have alcohol problems prior to their arrival. This is also true for older immigrants addicted to illicit substances. Young immigrants between the ages of 15-25, however, tend to acquire their alcohol or drug problems after immigration. The risk of young immigrants becoming drug abusers is said to be at least twice as high as for native born Germans (Riecken, 1999).

United States

According to the U.S. Immigration and Naturalization Service (1998), almost 400,000 people from the FSU arrived in the United States since 1986. The largest contingent of the immigrants was from Ukraine and Russia, and most settled in or around major metropolitan areas of New York, Philadelphia, Chicago, Cleveland, St. Louis, Los Angeles and parts of Northern California and Texas. There is no documentation available on the prevalence of alcohol and drug problems among these immigrants.

In the absence of official documentation, it appears anecdotally that a large portion of FSU immigrants in the United States are of Jewish background. As indicated previously, Jews in the United States and other western countries are believed to have a lower rate of alcoholism or alcohol dependence than the general population (Straussner, 2001c).

TABLE 3. A Comparison of Drug Abusers from FSU and Native Germans

Substance	Immigrants from FSU	Native Germans
Prevalence of Illicit Drug Use:		
Ever used	N/A	27%
Last year	N/A	5%
Treatment Population:		
Dependent on drugs	4-6%	> 1%
Proportion of Men	50%	75%
Proportion of Women	50%	25%
Alcohol abuse/dependence	2%	3%
mean age of alcohol abusing		
patients	43	43

Sources: Bundeszentrale fuer gesundheitliche Aufklaerung, 2001; Buehringer et al. 1997

Published rates of alcohol dependence among Jews in the United States range from 2 to 8 percent (Bailey, Haberman & Alksne, 1965; Bainwol & Gressard, 1985), with an estimated prevalence of 3 percent (Straussner, 2001c). In contrast, the general population has an estimated 10 percent rate of alcohol dependence. The use of illicit drugs among Jewish Americans, however, appears to be similar to or slightly higher than the population at large (Straussner, 2001c).

An analysis of 138 clients seen during 2000-2001 in one specialized out-patient substance abuse treatment program in New York City serving the immigrant FSU community, revealed the following characteristics (Kagan, personal communication, June, 2001):

- 84% of the clients were male, and 16% female, a ratio of men to women somewhat similar to drug abusing immigrants found in Israel, but not among FSU immigrants in Germany
- The mean age of clients was 33 years, with 20% under the age of 21
- The primary drugs that were abused were:
  Heroin/other opiates–56%
  Alcohol–33%
  Crack/cocaine–2%
  Other drugs (e.g. marijuana, club drugs)–8%
- Seventeen percent (17%) were diagnosed as polysubstance abusers;
- Over a quarter (26%) of the substance abusers were dually diagnosed with another psychiatric disorder;

- Thirteen percent (13%) of the clients were homeless;
- The majority (61%) of the clients had lived in the United States for 3 to 10 years; 21% have been there for 1-3 years; 17% for more than 10 years, and one percent (1%) arrived less than one year ago.

DISCUSSION

Despite widespread recognition of alcohol and drug abuse problems among immigrants from the FSU, little knowledge exists regarding their characteristics, treatment needs, treatment outcomes and effective prevention approaches. Studies in Israel and Germany indicate that many of these immigrants had an alcohol and/or drug abuse problem prior to their migration. Data on this point among FSU immigrants to the U.S. are not available. These and other findings need to be examined in a more systematic way that will permit comparison between substance abusers who are still living in the FSU with those who emigrated.

Among the issues that have been identified by clinicians and researchers in the U.S., Germany and Israel as having particular salience for FSU immigrants are: treatment barriers, including client views toward treatment; special medical needs; issues related to substance abuse among FSU women, issues related to substance abuse professionals, including social work; and policy issues.

Treatment Barriers

Despite the availability of well-developed treatment systems in Israel, Germany and the United Stated, there appear to be various barriers to the utilization of treatment that are particular to FSU immigrants resulting in apparent underutilization of treatment, particular by those with alcohol problems, and treatment resistance by individuals who are already in treatment. These barriers include: high mistrust of government institutions; a pervasive view of substance abuse as a moral problem rather than a disease; strong resistance to seeking professional help; and reluctance to participate in treatment and support approaches that require quasi-public revelation, such as group therapy and 12 step programs (i.e., Alcoholics or Narcotics Anonymous). Language barriers and lack of insurance may further contribute to the avoidance of addressing the problem of substance abuse in this population. Moreover, lack of awareness and understanding of substance abuse treatment, particularly for alcohol dependence, by family members, Russian-speaking professionals, and community leaders results in an insufficient network of significant people who can influence, refer and motivate the drug abuser to undertake treatment (Kagan & Shafer, 2001). In addition, since the use of methadone treatment is illegal in Russia, this may impact on the FSU heroin users' willingness to seek such treatment, and on their treatment compliance once in treatment.

According to clinical observations in Germany, the attitude of FSU immigrants toward drug dependence and how it should be treated reflects a culturally determined "construction of reality." Immigrants from FSU are more likely to see the detoxification process as the total treatment, something that is quick and effective, rather than as the beginning of a long recovery process. Moreover, they tend to view the clients' role as passively "enduring" treatment and not requiring their active participation (Schwichtenberg & Weig, 1999).

What little is known about substance abusing immigrants from the FSU in the United States also reveals that they are generally not interested or willing to participate in therapy, especially traditional substance abuse counseling (Kagan & Shafer, 2001). In addition to their historically high mistrust of government, this may also be the result of fear of affecting their migration status in the United States if they are identified as abusing an illegal substance (Kagan, 1997).

It is worth noting the continuing use by the FSU immigrants in Israel of alcohol and/or drugs while attending heroin treatment programs, and their belief that they could stop their drug use if they so wanted. Such views may indicate a treatment population that is much less likely to recover and one that may require a different treatment approach.

Medical Needs

Given the limited access to good medical care in the FSU, special attention must be paid to the medical needs of this population. High rate of tuberculosis, exposure to HIV, to hepatitis C, and to nuclear radiation have all been identified among immigrants from the FSU (Belkin, 1999; Chemtob, Leventhal & Weiler-Ravell, 2002; Perez Foster, 2001). These health issues need to be recognized among the substance abusing population and appropriate treatment needs to be provided.

Issues Related to Substance Abuse Among FSU Women

The prevalence rate of alcohol and other drug abuse among women in the general FSU population, or among FSU women immigrants is currently unknown. Data from Israel, Germany and the United States reveals that women constitute from 15 to 22% of substance abusing FSU immigrants in treatment. The findings in Germany that women constitute 50% of the FSU treatment population are highly unusual and need to be explored further (see Table 4).

Because prostitution is a common means of obtaining money for drugs, particular concern needs to be raised about the spread of HIV and hepatitis C among this population as well as those who have sexual contact with them.

Violence may be an additional risk factor for women from the FSU. Clinical observations in the United States and in Russia (Kagan & Shaefer, 2001; Straussner, personal observations, 2001) as well as preliminary research findings from Israel (Isralowitz and Bar Hamburger, 2002) reveal a high degree of domestic violence among this population. Much more research needs to be done on this subject and comparisons to other ethnocultural groups can further illuminate this dynamic and its relationship to substance abuse.

Issues Related to Substance Abuse Treatment Professionals

Historically, substance abuse treatment and the role of treatment professionals in the FSU differed greatly from their Western counterparts (see Kagan & Shafer, 2001). Such differences continue today and most substance abuse professionals in the FSU trained as psychiatrists who specialized in "addictionology." The Western notion of substance abuse counselors and the role of social workers are still foreign to the FSU, although Russia and Ukraine are in the midst of major social and professional changes, which attempt to incorporate Western views and treatment approaches (Anderson, 1992).

Policy Issues

From the perspective of drug treatment policies, a major challenge remains in terms of how best to address the needs of addicts with cul-

TABLE 4. Proportion of FSU Men and Women in Treatment in Different Countries

Country	Men	Women
Germany	50	50
Israel	80	20
U.S.	84	16

turally distinct background characteristics. While separate programs for substance abusing immigrants from different ethnic groups may be indicated, researchers have not provided compelling evidence that separate programs for immigrants or substance abusers from different ethnic or cultural groups are superior to mainstream efforts. Experts question the cost-effectiveness of such 'special' programs and caution clinicians that they must be wary of defining any patient in relation only to ethnic or racial group membership, especially since other patient-related variables, such as addiction severity, employment stability, criminal involvement, education level, and socioeconomic status, have been found to have greater implications for successful outcomes (Isralowitz & Bar Hamburger, 2002; Sullivan & Fleming, 1997). Nonetheless, clinical observations indicate that treatment of special populations may be enhanced if their particular needs are considered and met (American Psychiatric Association, 1995; Institute of Medicine, 1990; Landry, 1996; Sullivan & Fleming, 1997). Thus, future research must examine the need and value of ethnocultural specific treatment and prevention programs and the particular and unique needs, if any, of this population.

CONCLUSION

This paper is a beginning effort to explore substance abuse issues among a large immigrant population with a known past and recent history of heavy use of alcohol and other drugs. Additional systematic research is essential if we are to provide effective prevention and treatment services to the many immigrants from the former Soviet Union. In addition, cross-national studies of immigrants from one nationality, with a comparison group in their homeland, can provide valuable data that may be applicable to other substance abusing immigrant groups throughout the world. We need to find out what factors in different countries impact on the abuse of substances, what culturally relevant specific experiences promote or prevent the use of substances, what services are available to meet the unique needs of a given population, and how can existing services be tailored to better meet those needs. Much research remains to be done to answer these and related questions and clinicians need to be better trained to work more effectively with this population.

REFERENCES

American Psychiatric Association (1995). *Practice guide for treatment of patients with substance use disorders: Alcohol, cocaine, opioids.* Washington, D.C.: Author

Anderson, D. (1992, August 4). Hazelden report: Russia hopes to adapt Western treatment methods. *Star Tribune*, p. 8E.

Bade, K. & Oltmer, J. (1999). Einfuehrung: Aussiedlerzuwanderung und Aussiedlerintegration. In K. Bade & J. Oltmer (Ed.). *Aussiedler: deutsche Einwanderer aus Osteuropa.* (pp 9-51). Osnabrueck: IMIS,

Bailey, H., Haberman, P. & Alksne, H. (1965). The epidemiology of alcoholism in an urban residential area. *Quarterly Journal for the Study of Alcohol*, 26: 19-40.

Bainwol, S. & Gressard, C. (1985). The incidence of Jewish alcoholism: A review of the literature. *Journal of Drug Education*, 15 (3): 217-223.

Bar Hamburger, R. (2001, July). Informal estimate of heroin addict population in Israel. Jerusalem: Israeli Anti-Drug Authority.

Belkin, L. (1999, May 30). A Brutal Cure, *New York Times Magazine*, p. 36.

Boos-Nuenning, U., Siefen, R., Kirkcalsy, B. Otyakmaz, B., & Surall, D. (2002*). Migration Und Sucht, Expertise im Auftrag des Buhdesministeriums fur Gesundheit.* Baden-Baden: Nomos.

Buehringer, G., Adelsberger, F., Heinemann, A., Kirschner, J., Knauss, I., Kraus, L. Pueschel, K. & Simon, R. (1997). 1997 Update on Methods and Figures about the Extent of the Drug Problem in Germany. *Sucht, 43, Special Edition 2*

Bundeszentrale fuer Gesundheitliche Aufklaerung (Ed) (2001) Die Drogenaffinitaet Jungendlicher in der Bundesrepublik Deutschland 2001. Keoln: BzGA.

Chemtov, D., Leventhal, A., & Weiler-Ravel, D. (2002). Tuberculosis in Israel-main Epidemiological Aspects *Journal of the Israel Medical Association*, 141(3): 226-232.

Chtenguelov, V. (2002). *Ukrainian perspective on substance abuse and some related issues.* Kiev (Ukraine): Ukrainian Research Institute on Social & Forensic Psychiatry and Substance Abuse, unpublished report.

Davis, R. (1994). Drug and alcohol use in the former Soviet Union. *International Journal of Addictions*, 19 (3), 141-152.

Dill, H., Frick, U., Hoefer, R., Kloever, B. & Straus, F. (2002) *Risikoverhalten junger Migrantinnen und Migranten. Expertise fuer das Bundesministerium fuer Gesundheit.* Baden-Baden: Nomos.

Eichenhofer, E. (1999). Migration und Recht. In E. Eichenhofer (Ed.) *Migration und Illegaliaet* (pp. 29-40). Osnabruek: IMIS.

Elisha, D. (1998). Israel Ministry of Health, Substance Abuse Treatment Unit: An Overview. In Isralowitz, R. (Ed.). (1998). *Palestinian and Israeli People Against Drug Use: Problems, Policies and Programs. A Cooperative Effort to Address the Problem Through Communication, Cooperation and Coordination. Conference Proceedings.* Tel Aviv: Economic Cooperation Foundation.

Escobar, J., Hoyos, N., & Gara, M. (2000). Immigration and mental health: Mexican Americans in the United States. *Harvard Review of Psychiatry*, 8(2): 64-72.

Federal Government's Commission for Foreigners' Issues (2000): *Fact and Figures on the Situation of Foreigners in the Federal Republic of Germany.* Bonn: Author.

Glassner, B. & Berg, B. (1985). Jewish Americans and alcohol: Processes of avoidance and definition. In Bennett, L. & Ames, G. (Eds*), The American Experience with Alcohol: Contrasting Cultural Perspective* (93-107). NY: Plenum Press.

Goode, E. (1989). *Drugs in American Society*, 3rd Ed. New York: Knopf

Goodenow, C. & Espin, O. (1993). Identity choices in immigrant adolescent females. *Adolescence*, 28:109:173-184.

Hasin, D., Rahav, G., Meydan, J., & Newmark, Y. (1998). The drinking of earlier and more recent Russian immigrants to Israel: Comparison to other Israelis. *Journal of Substance Abuse*, 10(4): 341-53

Institute of Medicine (1990). *Broadening the base of treatment for alcohol problems.* Washington, D.C.: National Academy Press.

Isralowitz, R. (2002). The social context and reality of substance use in the Middle East. In Isralowitz, R., Afifi, M. & Rawson, R. (Ed.) *Drug Addiction: Cross Cultural Policy and Program Development* (pp. 11-24). Westport, CT: Auburn House.

Isralowitz, R. (2001). Toward an understanding of Russian speaking heroin addicts and drug treatment services. *Journal of Social Work Practice in the Addictions*, 1(2): 33-44.

Isralowitz, R., Abu Saad, I., & Telias, D. (1996). Work values among heroin addicts: A status model perspective *Journal of Offender Rehabilitation*, 24(1/2), 141-154.

Isralowitz, R. & Bar Hamburger, R. (2002). Immigrant and native-born female heroin addicts in Israel *Journal of Psychoactive Drugs*, 34(1): 97-103.

Isralowitz, R. & Borkin, S. (2002). Russian-speaking immigrants: Factors associated with heroin use. In Isralowitz, R. Afifi, M. & Rawson, R. (Eds.). *Drug Problems: Cross-Cultural Policy and Program Development*, (pp. 89-112). Westport, CT: Auburn House

Isralowitz, R., Telias, D. & Abu Saad, I. (1994). Psychological characteristics of heroin addicts and non-drug users in Israel: A status model comparison. *Journal of Social Psychology*, 134(3): 399-401.

Isralowitz, R., Telias, D., & Zighelbaum, Y. (1992). Heroin addiction in Israel: A comparison of addicts in prison, community-based facilities, and non-drug users based on selected psychological factors. *International Journal of Offender Therapy and Comparative Criminology*, 36(1): 62-72.

James, D. (1997). Coping with a new society: The unique psychosocial problems of immigrant youth. *Journal of School Health*, 67(3): 98-102.

Kagan, H. (1997, May). *The unique experiences of the family oriented treatment program for Russian substance abusers.* Paper presented at the annual National Association of Social Workers Alcoholism Institute, New York City.

Kagan, H. & Shafer, K. (2001). Russian-speaking substance abusers in transition. In S. L.A. Straussner, (Ed.). *Ethnocultural Factors in Substance Abuse Treatment* (pp. 250-271). New York: Guilford.

Keller, M. (1970). The great Jewish drink mystery. *British Journal of Addictions*. 64: 287-296.

Kraus, L. & Augustin, R. (2001). Population Survey on the Consumption of Psychoactive Substances in the German Adult Population 2000. *Sucht 47, Special Edition 1.*

Krupinski, J. (1984). Changing patterns of migration to Australia and their influence on the health of migrants, *Social Science & Medicine*, 18 (11): 927-37.

Landry, M. (1996). *Overview of addiction treatment effectiveness*. Washington, :D.C.: DHHS Publication (SMA) Rockville, MD: USDHHS

Monteiro, M. G., Klein, J. L., & Schuckit, M. A. (1991). High levels of sensitivity to alcohol in young adult Jewish men: A pilot study. *Journal of Studies on alcohol* 52(5):464-469.

Oetting, E.R. & Beauvais, F. (1990). Orthogonal cultural identification theory: The cultural identification of minority adolescents. *International Journal of the Addictions*. 25 (5/6): 655-685.

Orlandi, M. (1995) The challenge of evaluating community-based prevention programs: A cross-cultural perspective, in M. Orlandi (Ed.), *Cultural Competence for Evaluators*, DHHS Pub. No. (SMA) 95-3066. Rockville, MD: USDHHS

Ortega, A., Rosenbeck, R., Alegria, M., & Desai, R. (2000). Acculturation and the lifetime risk of psychiatric and substance use disorders among Hispanics. *Journal of Nervous Mental Disorders*. 188(11): 728-35.

Perez Foster, R. M (2000). Russian immigrants in the United States: Understanding the legacy of nuclear trauma. Paper presented at the annual conference of the New York State Psychological Association, Radisson Hotel, June 12.

Powles, J., Macaskill, G., Hopper, J., & Ktenas, D. (1991). Differences in drinking patterns associated with migration from a Greek island to Melbourne, Australia: A study of sibships. *Journal of Studies on Alcohol* 52 (3): 224-31.

Riecken, A. (1999). *Migration und psychiatrische Erkrankungen*. Osnabrueck (MA-thesis, Unpublished).

Rogler, L., Cortes, D. & Malgady, R. (1991). Acculturation and mental health status among Hispanics. *American Psychologist*. 46(6): 585-597.

Schmid, M. (2002). *Migration, Drogenkonsum und Drogenhilfe: Empirische Grundlagen und Konsequenzen fuer die Drogenhilfe*. NRW: Landeszentrum fuer Zuwanderung.

Schwichtenberg, U. & Weig, W. (1999): Die Behandlung von illegalen Drogen abhaengiger Aussiedler in einem Niedersaechsischem Landeskrankenaus. In R. Salman, S. Tuna & A. Lessing (Eds.): *Handbuch interkulturelle Suchthilfe* (pp. 184-190), Giessen: Psychosozial Verlag.

Segal, B. (1990). *The drunken society: Alcohol abuse and alcoholism in the Soviet Union*. New York: Hippocrene Books.

"Smoking Shortens Life Expectancy of Russian Men" (2002, August, 25). *Washington Post*, A1.

Spector, M. (1997a, November 9). A drug plague boils out of Russia's kitchens." *New York Times*, Sec 4, p.5.

Spector, M. (1997b, November 4). At a western outpost of Russia, AIDS spreads like a forest fire. *New York Times*, A1, p.10.

Straussner, S. L. A (2001a) (Ed.). *Ethnocultural factors in substance abuse treatment*. New York: Guilford.

Straussner, S. L. A. (2001b) (Ed.). Ethnocultural issues in substance abuse treatment: An overview. In Straussner, S. L. A.(Ed.). *Ethnocultural Factors in Substance Abuse Treatment* (pp. 3-28). New York: Guilford.

Straussner, S. L. A. (2001c). Jewish substance abusers: existing but invisible. In Straussner, S. L. A. (Ed.). *Ethnocultural Factors in Substance Abuse Treatment* (pp. 291-317) New York: Guilford.

Strobl, M. & Kuehnel, W. (2000). *Dazugehoerig und ausgegrenzt. Analysen zu Integrationsschancen junger Aussiedler.* Weinheim: Juventa.

Sullivan, E. & Fleming, M. (1997). *A guide to substance abuse for primary care clinicians.* 97-3139, Rockville, MD: USDHHS.

Van Geest, J. & Johnson, T. (1997). Substance use patterns among homeless migrants and nonmigrants in Chicago. *Substance Use and Misuse,* 32 (7-8): 877-907.

Vogt, I. & Schmid, M. (2000). Crack-Konsum in der Drogenszene in Frankfurt am Main: Ergebnisse empirischer Studien. *Wiener Zeitschrift fuer Suchtforschung,* 23: 5-13.

Westermeyer, J. J. (1993). Substance use disorders among young minority refugees: Common themes in a clinical sample. In De La Rosa, M.R. & Recio Adrados, J-L, (Eds.). *Drug Abuse Among Minority Youth: Advances in Research and Methodology* (pp. 308-320). NIDA Research Monograph 130. Rockville, MD: USDHHS.

Wright, P. (1994, Sept.). Following specific guidelines will help you assess cultural competence in program design, application and management, *Prevention Works: Technical Assistance Bulletin.* Rockville, MD: NCADI.

SPECIAL TOPICS

Legalization of Drugs:
Perspectives from the United States,
United Kingdom, and Australia

Elizabeth Zelvin
Jim Barber
Bill Coleman
Philip Guy

Moderator: Elizabeth Zelvin

America, Britain, and Australia are all nations with great commonality of language and political traditions, but each has dealt with the legal aspect of substance abuse in a way that reflects its particular culture. In the United States, we tried making alcohol illegal in the Prohibition era from 1919 to 1932, and found that we

Jim Barber, PhD, BSW, BA, is Professor of Social Work at the School of Social Administration & Social Work, Flinders University, Adelaide, South Australia and Director of the Australian Centre for Community Services Research. Bill Coleman, CSW, CP, PAT, currently works as a Psychodramatist at Four Winds Hospital in Katonah, New York and is on the Faculty at Hudson Valley Psychodrama Institute in New Paltz, New York. Philip Guy, BA, MASW, is Lecturer in Social Work and Addictions, Department of Social Work at the University of Hull, UK. Elizabeth Zelvin, CSW, ACSW, CASAC, C-CATODSW, is Special Topics Editor of *Journal of Social Work Practice in the Addictions*, and a psychotherapist who practices online at <www.LZcybershrink.com>.

[Haworth co-indexing entry note]: "Legalization of Drugs: Perspectives from the United States, United Kingdom, and Australia." Zelvin et al. Co-published simultaneously in *Journal of Social Work Practice in the Addictions* (The Haworth Social Work Practice Press, an imprint of The Haworth Press, Inc.) Vol. 2, No. 3/4, 2002, pp. 137-144; and: *International Aspects of Social Work Practice in the Addictions* (ed: Shulamith Lala Ashenberg Straussner, and Larry Harrison) The Haworth Social Work Practice Press, an imprint of The Haworth Press, Inc., 2002, pp. 137-144. Single or multiple copies of this article are available for a fee from The Haworth Document Delivery Service [1-800-HAWORTH, 9:00 a.m. - 5:00 p.m. (EST). E-mail address: getinfo@haworthpressinc.com].

merely succeeded in criminalizing the production and distribution of alcoholic beverages and creating an underground subculture around the speakeasy. In recent years, our government's War on Drugs has focused on the supply side of illicit drugs, including heroin, cocaine, and marijuana, with debatable success and a growing movement in opposition, especially regarding marijuana. What is the current situation in your country?

Guy: In the UK, alcohol became a more regulated substance and cocaine and opium became illicit substances as an emergency and temporary measure during the First World War. Despite the initial success of supply-side measures in reducing alcohol consumption and related harm, their impact gradually diminished, until by the 1990s the rates of problems had returned to 1914 levels. A relaxation of alcohol regulation occurred after industry lobbying in 1992. The relaxation of controls has done nothing to stem the rise of alcohol consumption and related problems.

Over the years, more substances have joined the illicit list. The UK has some of the highest penalties for drug possession and drug dealing in the world. The maximum sentence for possession of a class A drug (mostly heroin and cocaine) is 7 years imprisonment, and for dealing, 21 years. These sentences exist in theory only: they are hardly ever imposed. The UK also has Europe's highest consumption figures. We consume about 30 tons of illicit heroin per year.

Most enforcement activity is directed at cannabis possession. In the UK cannabis is currently a 'class B' drug. Possession can carry a penalty of up to 5 years in prison. In every year since the law was created over 75%, and sometimes up to 90%, of all drug offenders have been arrested for cannabis possession. It is being suggested now that this is not an efficient use of resources and effort should be redirected towards heroin and cocaine. The proposal is to down-grade cannabis to 'class C.' This would mean that possession would remain outside of the law but it would not carry a prison sentence and it would be a non arrestable offense, like parking a car in a prohibited place. In the UK the enforcement agencies claim to intercept approximately 10% of the illegal drug market. As far as I am aware, no country claims to achieve more than a 30% success rate, so most drug activity is free of state control.

Barber: Prior to federation in 1900, Australia consisted of separate states, several of which had already prohibited the smoking of opium. At this time, the practice of smoking opium was a pastime of the Chinese working mainly in Australia's frenetic gold fields. Drug laws were expanded soon after federation and at the 1925 Geneva Convention, Australia agreed to limit to medical and scientific purposes the manufacture and use of opium, cocaine, morphine, Indian hemp, and heroin. During the first half of the twentieth century, the occasional case of opioid dependence was managed by medical practitioners who could authorize prescription of opiods if all efforts to encourage the user to quit had failed.

By 1951, Australia was reported to have the highest rate of per capita heroin consumption in the world, but adverse effects, measured in terms of health and crime indicators, were low. Nevertheless, international pressure was brought to bear on Australia via the World Health Organization to outlaw the use of heroin altogether. Over the objections of the Australian Medical Association, a total prohibition on importation and production of heroin was imposed by the Commonwealth of Australia in 1953. At first, it seemed that heroin use might die out altogether in Australia, but when Australian and US servicemen from the Vietnam War began visiting Australian cities (especially Sydney) for rest and recreation in the 1960s, many soldiers brought with them the heroin that was so plentiful and cheap in the Golden Triangle of Southeast Asia. Over the years that followed, heroin use spread rapidly throughout the nation.

Australia officially adopted a national policy of "harm minimization" at a Premiers' Conference held in Canberra in April 1985. The meeting was convened by the Prime Minister of Australia and was attended by all State Premiers and Chief Ministers. Curiously, the term "harm minimization" was never defined at the Conference but one tangible outcome of the meeting was funding for needle and syringe exchanges and methadone maintenance programs. Government policy makers came to regard such initiatives as living proof of Australia's enlightened approach to illicit drug regulation and pointed with pride at the very low rate of HIV and Hepatitis C infection compared with cities like New York, which pursued a policy of "zero tolerance." In reality, however, Australia is now and has been for decades "tough on drugs." For most of this century, the trend in Australia has been towards: (a) subjecting more substances to prohibitions and controls, (b) increasing the scope and number of offenses and making them easier to prove in court, (c) increasing the severity of statutory penalties, and (d) extending the enforcement and investigative powers of the police.

Seemingly unaware of the inconsistency with the country's avowed policy of harm minimization, for example, the Prime Minister of Australia, John Howard, publicly endorsed a zero tolerance approach to illicit drug use in 1998, even though his Ministerial Council on Drug Strategy had reiterated its commitment to harm minimization at much the same time. In financial terms, Australia currently commits around 84% of its expenditure on the war on drugs to law enforcement. A mere 6% and 10% are allocated to treatment and to prevention and research respectively. If Australia truly has a policy of harm minimization, it is not manifested by putting its money where its mouth is. Moreover, recent attempts by non-government drug treatment agencies to conduct a heroin trial were thwarted by the Federal Government, with the Prime Minister himself bawling out in Parliament House that, "Australia will never have a heroin trial as long as I am Prime Minister of this country."

Coleman: This is an immensely complex issue. On the Internet, the search engine Google comes up with 42,600 hits for "legalization of drugs." It would make a fascinating research project to see what statistics these many thousands of references reveal. The government tells us that research shows that most Americans are against legalization of drugs. Yet it is difficult to find such a consensus in any informal group one might survey. I have great respect for research, but I know that the conclusions of any research must be seen *only* in light of the structure of the research.

The US Department of Justice (2001) has published a thought-provoking list of questions to be asked regarding legalization of drugs:

- Should all drugs be legalized?
- Who will determine which segments of the population will have access to legalized drugs?
- Will they be limited only to people over 18? Over 21?
- Will cocaine, heroin, LSD, or PCP be made available if people request them?
- Who will sell drugs, the government? Private companies?
- Who will be liable for damages caused by drug use, and the activities of those taking drugs?
- Who will collect the revenues generated by the drug sales?
- How will cheaper drugs on the black market be controlled?
- Who will bear the costs to society of increased drug use?
- How will absenteeism and loss of productivity be addressed by business?
- Will the local drug situation in a community dictate which drugs are sold where?

- How will society care for and pay for the attendant social cost of increased drug use, including family disintegration and child neglect?
- Who will bear the costs of the expansion of social service and welfare programs that may be necessary to care for increased drug addiction through drug legalization?
- Would taxpayers bear this expense through increased taxes? Would funding for other programs such as education be reduced?
- Will people still need prescriptions for currently controlled medications, such as antibiotics, if drugs are legalized?
- Will legal drugs require prescriptions?
- Can anyone, regardless of physical or medical conditions, purchase drugs?
- How will we deal with the influx of people to the United States who will seek legal drugs?
- Can we begin a legalization program in your neighborhood for one year?

Barber: Many of these are purely rhetorical questions, of course, and the fact remains that, at least in Australia, results of our predilection for law enforcement are not impressive. The Australian National Council on AIDS and Related Diseases, for example, estimates that the number of injecting drug users in this country has increased at the rate of around 7% per annum since the 1960s. Furthermore, all of the known indicators of illicit drug misuse are moving in the wrong direction: the number of drug seizures is rising, as is the number of overdose deaths and drug-related crime rates such as armed robbery and burglary. Meanwhile, the age of persons arrested for drug-related offenses is falling, as is the age of persons attending syringe exchanges. Such trends suggest that the "tough on drugs" emphasis has more to do with public opinion polls than containing the misery wrought by drug addiction. As Switzerland and the Netherlands discovered in the 1990s, however, there are other options. By shifting public investment away from supply-side strategies towards demand-side policies and harm minimization initiatives, like prescription heroin and safe injecting rooms, these countries managed to reverse some very alarming trends in drug-related strife.

Coleman: As a former U.S. federal Special Agent and currently as a social worker often treating substance abusers, I have come full circle several times about what is needed. When I come across a young person in his or her twenties serving a long prison sentence for selling small quantities of marijuana to friends, I ache with grief and can see no justice at work. When I treat an adolescent who was high on Ecstasy and LSD and ran a car off the road, killing the passengers, I am enraged at those who produced and distributed the mood-altering substances and want to demand that they be locked up forever. We in the United States have not discussed this topic publicly nearly enough. We can see that the results in countries that have enacted legislation decriminalizing drugs are not enviable. There has always been a cost to society. Can we even begin to calculate the cost in the U.S., the world's biggest drug market ever?

I am clearly on the side of anti-legalization–at this time. But, I also want to decriminalize the personal use of mood-altering substances. I don't believe we are prepared, as a nation, to permit the free flow of drugs. The examples are many. Do you want your baby sitter high on marijuana? How about your tax accountant strung out on cocaine? Or factory workers taking a heroin break? Yet it makes little sense to expect the criminal justice system to provide a long term answer. There is some evidence to show that drug prevention and demand reduction are working, however slowly. Our efforts should be doubled and redoubled.

Barber: Yes, I agree with you entirely. One only needs to look at what has been achieved with legal drugs. Over the last couple of decades or so, restrictions on tobacco sponsorship of sport combined with highly visible public health campaigns and legislative restrictions on advertising and availability coincided with a 15% reduction in lifetime smoking prevalence rates in Australia between 1985 and 1995. And the decision to tackle alcohol under the National Campaign Against Drug Abuse saw the proportion of non-drinkers in the Australian population rise from 15% in 1988 to 20% only 7 years later. The proportion of heavy drinkers also declined during this time, as did the age of initiation to alcohol. Importantly, all of this was achieved by focusing only on demand-side strategies.

Guy: From 1926 the UK had what many regard as a highly successful drug policy. Known as "The British System," it consisted of doctors prescribing heroin and cocaine to users. Heroin is still a widely prescribed drug used for pain relief. A small number of addicts also continue to receive prescriptions. The wide scale prescribing of heroin came to an end in 1968 for political reasons when a handful of doctors were found to over-prescribe these substances for profit. This could have been curtailed through tightened procedures. Appearing tough was an act of populism on the part of government. Our current government is now proposing that we return to the prescription of heroin for some drug addicts.

Zelvin: Jim (Barber), you contrasted the "harm minimization" in Australia to New York's policy of zero tolerance. In fact, with New York's high incidence of HIV infection, we have had needle exchange programs. For us, that was exactly where the idea of harm reduction originated. This concept has affected how we conceptualize alcohol and drug addictions in general and even where the funding for treatment goes, at least in New York.

Coleman: Outside New York, most of the prominent American treatment centers, including Hazelden, Sierra Tucson, Betty Ford, and Mountainside, to name a few, generally follow a 12-step or AA oriented model and a treatment philosophy of total abstinence as the universal goal. This must not be mistaken for an oversimplification. There is something much deeper embedded in this model. The underlying philosophy is to nurture a way of life where it is not *necessary* or even *desirable* to take a drink or a drug. This is often accomplished in the closed container offered by AA and treatment centers that borrow its approach. Yet it takes years of practice before members are comfortable in their own skins without the assistance of mood altering substances. The question is how do we extend such a treatment philosophy to the populace at large without mandating spirituality by insisting that people believe in a higher power and in complete surrender. Maybe we can't. But I see little hope in the alternatives.

Zelvin: In general, what do you think your country needs?

Barber: What is needed most in Australia is a redefinition of drug addiction as a health and social issue rather than criminal behavior. In particular, cultivation, production, distribution, sale or possession of small quantities of illicit drugs consistent with personal use should not involve criminal sanction. While certain illicit drug activities such as unauthorized trafficking, need to remain a crime, there should be more emphasis on non-custodial sentences for drug users wherever possible so that they can be diverted into treatment programs. There is also no logical reason why the production and sale of cannabis should remain a crime. In fact, moves in this direction have already begun in my home state of South Australia where expiation of cannabis charges on payment of a fine was introduced back in 1986. Finally, it should also be apparent from what I have already said that I am an advocate for a more balanced allocation of funding between law enforcement, prevention and treatment.

Guy: The UK is a multicultural society. I cannot accept the UK's current drug laws because they produce a racist outcome. People from Black African, Black Caribbean, or Asian backgrounds are less likely to use or trade in drugs than those of White European origin. Yet non-whites are more likely to be stopped in the street and searched under our drug laws. They also are more likely to be arrested, more likely to be charged, less likely to be given bail, and more likely to be convicted. They also are more likely to receive a prison sentence. That sentence is likely to be longer, and parole is less likely to be granted. It is not clear to me that one form of intoxication is worse than any other. In my view, we need laws that tell our people what they can do, rather than what they cannot. These laws should be properly constructed and have robust safeguards.

Coleman: Beyond our prevention and demand reduction efforts, we can reduce drug consumption through enough social pressure, or better yet, through "social capital." Putnam (2000) describes social capital, or features of social organization, such as networks, norms, and social trust, that facilitate coordination and cooperation for mutual benefit. He says "life is easier in a community blessed with a substantial stock of social capital" (Putnam, 1995, p. 67). I would add that while our social capital has been declining, our drug problem has been escalating. How do we build this social capital? Criminalizing drug abuse is a poor way to motivate a society to change. For example, it has been thoroughly established that capital punishment does not deter capital crimes. Drug and alcohol abuse and dependence have become social norms. We cannot reverse such norms through legalization of drugs. Please consider what kind of message that would be to children. The real questions should be concerned with those norms. Do we want a society in which members can get high at will and with complete impunity? We are not ready to legalize drugs. We do need to double and redouble our prevention and treatment effort. We also need to do a lot of work at the community level before we make such a leap into the unknown.

REFERENCES

Putnam, R.D. (2000). *Bowling alone: The collapse and revival of American community.* New York: Touchstone/Simon & Schuster.

Putnam, R.D. (1995). "Bowling alone: America's declining social capital." *Journal of Democracy* 6:1 65-78.

U.S. Dept. of Justice, Drug Enforcement Administration, Demand Reduction Section. (2001) "Speaking out against legalization of drugs." Available at: <www.usdoj.gov/dea/demand/druglegal/index.html>.

ENDPAGE

A Shooting Gallery in Germany

Printed with Permission. Photo by Dr. Lala Straussner, July, 2001.

An injection room in Frankfurt, Germany where intravenous drug users are provided with sterile works that allow them to inject drugs in a supervised, safe environment. Users have to be at least 18 years of age and can stay in the room up to 30 minutes at a time.

Social workers and medical staff are available for anyone who wants or needs social or medical services. The opening of such injection rooms has resulted in significant reduction of drug-related deaths and HIV transmission in the city.

[Haworth co-indexing entry note]: "Endpage." Co-published simultaneously in *Journal of Social Work Practice in the Addictions* (The Haworth Social Work Practice Press, an imprint of The Haworth Press, Inc.) Vol. 2, No. 3/4, 2002, p. 145; and: *International Aspects of Social Work Practice in the Addictions* (ed: Shulamith Lala Ashenberg Straussner, and Larry Harrison) The Haworth Social Work Practice Press, an imprint of The Haworth Press, Inc., 2002, p. 145. Single or multiple copies of this article are available for a fee from The Haworth Document Delivery Service [1-800-HAWORTH, 9:00 a.m. - 5:00 p.m. (EST). E-mail address: getinfo@haworthpressinc.com].

145

Index

Abstinence, as substance abuse
  treatment goal, 143
Abuse, 14
Academy of Certified Social Workers,
  23
Acamprosate, 18
Addictionology, 131
Addiction Technology Transfer
  Center, 19
Adolescents
  alcohol beverage sales to, 53
  alcohol use by, 70,71,72,108
  drug abuse by, 34
  drug prevention education for,
    107-109
  drug testing in, 11
  European School Survey Project on
    Alcohol and Other Drugs
    (ESPAD) for, 34
  inhalant abuse by, 98,101,122
  marijuana (cannabis) use by, 70,71
  walk-in clinics for, 92
Advocacy groups, for drug addicts, 79
Afghanistan, as opium/heroin supplier,
  122
African Americans, crack cocaine use
  by, 11
Aftercare services, for recovering
  substance abusers
  in Germany, 79
  in Singapore, 113-115
Age factors, in alcohol abuse, 72-73
Alcohol, as gateway drug, 108,115
Alcohol abuse. *See also* under specific
  countries
  age factors in, 72-73
  arrests for, 9
  familial, effect on substance abuse
    treatment outcome, 111

gender differences in, 72-73
in immigrants, 124,125,127
parental, 11,41,42,43,108
prevention campaigns, 142
public attitudes toward, 70
Alcohol consumption rate
  among adolescents, 53
  in Germany, 70,71
  in Israel, 86
  in Russia, 121-122
  in Singapore, 98,99-100
    among women, 98,99
  in the United Kingdom, 138
  world-wide increase in, 2
Alcoholic beverages, sale to
  minors, 53
Alcoholics
  day centers for, 90-91
  drug addicts' attitudes toward, 75
  lack of employment protection for,
    10
  lack of health care access by, 10
  recovering, counselor training for,
    93
Alcoholics Anonymous (AA),
    13,16,20-21,79,92
  spirituality component of, 20-21
Alcoholism. *See also* Alcohol abuse
  disease model of, 35-36,46
  genetic factors in, 16-17,112
  public health model of, 35
Alcoholism treatment. *See also*
    Detoxification programs
  gender differences in, 73
  inpatient, 35-36
    versus outpatient, 14,15
  Minnesota Model of, 36
  naltrexone as, 18,104
  psychiatric, 35-36

SPECIAL 25%-OFF DISCOUNT!

Order a copy of this book with this form or online at:
http://www.haworthpress.com/store/product.asp?sku=**4859**
Use Sale Code BOF25 in the online bookshop to receive 25% off!

International Aspects of Social Work Practice in the Addictions

____ in softbound at $14.96 (regularly $19.95) (ISBN: 0-7890-1997-3)
____ in hardbound at $29.96 (regularly $39.95) (ISBN: 0-7890-1996-5)

COST OF BOOKS _____

Outside USA/ Canada/
Mexico: Add 20% _____

POSTAGE & HANDLING _____
(US: $4.00 for first book & $1.50
for each additional book)
Outside US: $5.00 for first book
& $2.00 for each additional book)

SUBTOTAL _____

in Canada: add 7% GST _____

STATE TAX _____
(NY, OH, & MIN residents please
add appropriate local sales tax

FINAL TOTAL _____
(if paying in Canadian funds, convert
using the current exchange rate,
UNESCO coupons welcome)

☐ BILL ME LATER: ($5 service charge will be added)
(Bill-me option is good on US/Canada/
Mexico orders only; not good to jobbers,
wholesalers, or subscription agencies.)

☐ Signature _____

☐ Payment Enclosed: $ _____

☐ PLEASE CHARGE TO MY CREDIT CARD:

☐Visa ☐MasterCard ☐AmEx ☐Discover
☐Diner's Club ☐Eurocard ☐JCB

Account #_____

Exp Date_____

Signature_____
(Prices in US dollars and subject to
change without notice.)

PLEASE PRINT ALL INFORMATION OR ATTACH YOUR BUSINESS CARD

Name		
Address		
City	State/Province	Zip/Postal Code
Country		
Tel	Fax	
E-Mail		

May we use your e-mail address for confirmations and other types of information? ☐Yes ☐No
We appreciate receiving your e-mail address and fax number. Haworth would like to e-mail or
fax special discount offers to you, as a preferred customer. **We will never share, rent, or
exchange your e-mail address or fax number.** We regard such actions as an invasion of
your privacy.

Order From Your Local Bookstore or Directly From
The Haworth Press, Inc.
10 Alice Street, Binghamton, New York 13904-1580 • USA
Call Our toll-free number (1-800-429-6784) / Outside US/Canada: (607) 722-5857
Fax: 1-800-895-0582 / Outside US/Canada: (607) 771-0012
E-Mail your order to us: Orders@haworthpress.com

Please Photocopy this form for your personal use.
www.HaworthPress.com

BOF03